You were born to be. . .

Published

Eleven Laws for Getting Your Writing into Print *NOW!*

Tom Bird

The Tom Bird Method is a trademark of Tom Bird Seminars, Inc.

Requests for such permissions should be addressed to:
Sojourn, Inc.
P. O. Box 4306
Sedona, Arizona 86340
www.TomBird.com

Bird, Thomas J.
     You Were Born to Be. . . Published: The Eleven Laws for Getting Your Writing into Print Now!

Layout: J. L. Saloff
Photography: Mel Russell
Cover: Jane Perini
Fonts: Book Antiqua, Belwe, Tahoma, HelvCE

Paperback:
10 digit ISBN: 0-9789216-2-3
13 digit ISBN: 978-0-9789216-2-0

Hardcover:
10 digit ISBN: 0-9707258-6-8
13 digit ISBN: 978-0-9707258-6-8
Library of Congress Control Number: 2006907855

First Edition

Printed in the USA on acid free paper.

1.02

To my Students:
You are all born to be published and
I am here to help you along your path in
any way that I can. Thank you for all that
you have taught me through the years.

Contents

Introduction

I DON'T EXPECT YOU TO INITIALLY BELIEVE ANYTHING THAT is written in this book, and that I say with great authority and confidence because I know your situation so well.

For at one time, I too had been led astray by inappropriate so-called authorities on publishing, the books, the teachers, the classes, the conferences, magazines, other writers, etc, that caused me to severely question whether I would really ever see my work in print.

All during those challenging years I just kept wondering how I could have been blessed with a desire to publish without a route being offered to live it.

Finally, out of desperation, I decided to step boldly away from all which had so severely influenced me and to develop my own system for becoming the published author my soul called me to be. As I did so I could feel a Divine Presence guiding me, as if all that I had previously experienced had led me to take this step, not only for myself but for struggling writers everywhere. Much to my surprise, after sitting down a system for getting my work published was released through me in only minutes. Two weeks later that same system led me to the acquisition of my first literary agent, who four weeks later sold my first book for a price equivalent to three times my yearly salary as the Assistant Director of Publicity with the big league's Pittsburgh Pirates.

Shortly afterwards, I began offering what I had learned about both the publishing and writing process through classes offered at local colleges and universities.

Little did I know how many people actually wanted to write and publish. Because of the response to my classes, word spread and in no time I was offering courses at locales all across the country.

It was twenty-three years ago that I offered my first course. Since then I have made over 3,000 lecture appearances at over a hundred different colleges and universities and appeared before over 50,000 aspiring writers, tens of thousands of whom have used my methods to acquire the publication they desired.

Since my first class, some aspects of the publishing industry have changed, and I have adjusted my method to reflect those changes. However, the basic structure that led so many to where they wanted to be as writers remains the same, and it can do for you what it has done for both myself and so many others.

Again, you may discover that what you find in the following pages is different, maybe even vastly so, from what you had been doing or thought that you should be doing with your writing. If that's the case, that's good because you need a change, for what you have been doing obviously hasn't been working for you—if it were you wouldn't be reading this book.

As the result of reading this book, you will be offered everything you need to first find and then follow the route that has already been laid before all of us who were born to be published.

It is the supreme art of the teacher to awaken joy in creative expression and knowledge.

Albert Einstein

Success Story from Nancy A. Hagener

From: Nancy A. Hagener, Phoenix, Arizona
To: Tom Bird
Author: *The Dance of Defiance*, (Shamrock Books)

I've been a writer all my life really, but it wasn't until I met Tom Bird and took his Writer's Success Series seminar at Scottsdale Community College, that I released my author within.

Through Tom's inspiration and step-by-step plan, I was able to visualize my book—from its cover to a basic content—and begin the process of writing. Taking Tom's advice, I asked my family for the gift of time over the holiday. Two weeks of uninterrupted time to dedicate to my book! It was truly a spiritual experience as some days I would look back and read what flowed from my pen, and wonder, "Who wrote that?"

I've been blessed by Tom's enthusiasm and his sharing of insights into the world of successful writers. I've now published *The Dance of Defiance: A Mother and Son Journey with Oppositional Defiant Disorder* to positive reviews. More importantly, I've been told that my book has touched hearts and changed lives. I believe Tom would agree, that's what it's all about.

Law #1

Always write what you feel most strongly about despite the fact that doing so might feel uncomfortable at times.

NOW THAT'S AN ODD STATEMENT, ISN'T IT? IMAGINE SOMEone telling you to do something that makes you feel uncomfortable. That doesn't sound like good advice at all, does it? That is, of course, unless you take into consideration that what has made you feel comfortable hasn't yet led you where it is that you feel drawn to go. If that's the case, then breaking free of that pattern, and it is usually an uncomfortable feeling breaking free of any pattern, is a necessity in making the change you obviously have to make to go to where it is that you seek to go as a writer.

You see, amongst that massive amount of really bad advice out there on publishing is the widespread belief that a writer should write whatever it is that the market is buying. Outrageous! Nothing could be further from the truth.

What those who adhere to this belief don't realize is that what the market buys above anything else is the passion exuded by the writer, and how can you express that cutting-edge passion if you are writing about something you don't care about?

Simply put: What you care most about, that which exudes the greatest response from you, will release the most passion in your writing and make whatever it is you are writing most attractive to your potential readers. Period.

Great Literature is simply language charged with meaning to the utmost possible degree.

Ezra Pound

So my advice to you is to let your writing be the oasis away from all of the compromises you make in your life.

Maybe you have a good-paying, secure job but you don't love it, which is fine. But let that not be the case with your writing. Write only what you love and let the passion released by that love be your guide, and never, never compromise. Never! Again, let this be your one oasis away from all of that. No longer sell out yourself and what you truly want to write.

A student from Florida with whom I work on an individual basis came to this realization, and it changed not only who how she approached writing but her entire life as well. She came to this understanding through hearing a bestselling author speak at a local bookstore.

Before beginning to sign books, the author made a small presentation to his audience and answered some questions. In the course of his presentation the topic came up about how he had finally achieved his success after struggling as a writer for so long.

"I finally stopped listening to, and trying to adjust to, what everyone else wanted to me to write, and wrote only what I, myself, wanted to write. And that made all the difference. When I made the decision to write whatever I wanted to write, whether it got published or not, everything took off for me," he said.

You see, up until that time this well-known author had no idea that what the readers of the world wanted was more than just a topic covered. They wanted to experience the passion another felt for a topic, no matter what that subject may be, possibly because they wanted to feel the passion that they, were unable to feel.

What aspiring writers most need to understand is that their success as published authors is directly tied to their potential audience's ability to live vicariously through not necessarily the topics they choose to write about but the passion they feel for that topic. In fact, all the aspects of the method you are about to be exposed to are tested and proven over nearly a quarter century of use by tens of thousands of aspiring writers from all walks of life. But none of them will work for you unless you are writing from your heart, with the passion to which your readers–looking to live vicariously through someone's passion–will be magnetically drawn.

How do you find that passion, that purpose, that topic, that direction, that book, about which you should be writing? Go inside of yourself. Connect with your Author Within. For it is there that it exists.

How do you do that?

First of all, what it is that you are most drawn to write is not hard to find. In fact, it is inside you, just below the surface of your skin, and has been with you all of your life.

Secondly, if you have the time, I would suggest that you read my book *You Were Born to. . . Write* and perform the series of exercises within it to lead you to the topic for which you feel the most passion.

Thirdly, if you don't feel as if you have the time to do that, I offer you, in the following pages, a series of exercises to lead you in the proper direction.

Whichever route you choose to go though, you will discover what it is that you are truly being drawn to write. Again, even if upon opening this book you feel strongly that you know what it is that you are meant to write, still do the following exercises or, even better, read *You Were Born to. . . Write*. For the part of you that is frightened to death of you writing can be very deceiving and convincing, and will do whatever it has to do to draw you away from the change and exposure that success in this one area of your life can bring. And if you start off on the wrong track, even if you are able to somehow complete the writing of it, you will find publication to be an uphill climb, if not all together impossible.

So it is in your best and highest interests to do whatever you have to do to minimize any chance of that transpiring. This translates to taking the necessary steps to tune into what is truly fueling your desires, what you "feel" yourself being drawn to, not what you "think" you should be writing about. There is a huge difference between the two.

Back when you were a baby or very young child, your deepest, most expressive side—which is tied to what I refer to as your Author Within (AW)—was allowed to openly express itself through your AW. If you were happy, you laughed. If you were sad, you cried, and if you were mad, you screamed, yelled, threw something. During those early years, your parents and other family members were your whole world, and they applauded whatever you felt and whichever way you chose to express it.

However, as you got bigger and older, much of what was once appreciated in you was no longer seen as acceptable. Over time, you were taught to think as opposed to feel. The older you got the more this foreign form of living was expected of you, and your logical brain—or your Logical, Critical Mind (LCM) as I call it—disproportionately evolved as the controlling force in your life.

The first step in helping you make what was thought to be a necessary conversion came in the form of punishment or discipline for openly expressing the feelings of your AW as they came streaming through your Creative, Connected Mind (CCM).

Eventually, if for no other reason other than self-preservation from a society that was forcing you–at all costs–to live in the unnatural state of the LCM, a wall formed between your CCM and your LCM. At the center of this wall was a series of strong, knee-jerk responses that opposed your CCM and thus the inspirations of your AW. These knee-jerk responses eventually separated you from your CCM and the Divine and took you away from the natural, spontaneous expressions of your AW.

To discover what it is that your AW is trying to lead you to write, this wall, which separates you from your CCM, needs to be lowered, at least temporarily, so you can see what is on the other side. To dissolve it permanently and free your AW for good, I suggest that you read my book *You Were Born to... Write.*

For our present purposes, to find out or confirm what is trying to express itself through you, you will need a few hundred 3" x 5" index cards. The following exercise may take several sessions. However long it takes, I suggest that you stay with it until whatever it is that you are meant to write appears in the form of a skeletal outline on your index cards.

Before you get to that point though, most aspiring writers go through two preliminary phases. The initial phase focuses on a cathartic experience, where the fears, concerns, excuses, anger, and frustration of your LCM, which seeks only to protect you from the pain the non-acceptance your CCM and AW received as a child, are vented. This phase usually lasts for a few sessions of your work with the cards before moving into the second preliminary phase, during which aspects of your primary archetypes are released. If you are meant to write fiction, your archetypes will surface in the form of characters who will be introduced. If it is nonfiction that you should write, a much deeper understanding of your motivation for writing about that topic and the themes tied to it will surface. Immediately after the passing through of these two phases, an outline of what it is that you are being drawn to write will surface.

To defuse the controlling aspects of your LCM, which could keep you from gaining access to your AW, in which your motivation for writing is housed, follow the steps below each day until the outline of what it is that you are being drawn to write surfaces. You can continue to read through this book as you work through the phases with your index cards. Just don't put anything else from this book into play until you have received a crystal-clear vision of what it is that you are being drawn to write through its appearance as an outline on your index cards.

1. Set a time to write each day, even if this is during the early morning hours when everyone in your house is still asleep, when you will be undisturbed for an hour.

2. Before beginning to write each day, sit quietly, close your eyes, and take a few deep breaths, focusing primarily on exhaling as deeply as you can.

3. Then after a few minutes, start writing whatever you are feeling or thinking on the index cards.

4. Refrain from censoring anything. Capture on the cards whatever you are feeling or thinking.

5. It is very important to keep writing as fast as you can. Let your thoughts and feelings lead the way during this exercise.

6. After you have written on the index cards for at least your appointed hour, make an appointment for your next writing session. The more consistent the timing of your daily sessions, the better.

7. Repeat the above steps until the outline surfaces for whatever it is that you are meant to write.

A student of mine by the name of Cindi Gawne, who attended my classes at the University of Tennessee, was nice enough to share with me some journal listings she made while going through her experience with "the cards," which I felt would help you better understand the specific phases and purpose behind this essential step. Even though your response to the cards may vary, in general almost everyone who employs this method goes through the same three phases, just in his or her own way.

Cindi Gawne and "The Cards"

As I walked out of the classroom at the University of Tennessee that warm April afternoon, I was determined to pursue my passion for writing, but even more so, I felt determined to have what I felt I saw in you that day — true contentment, joy, the 'I'm glad to be alive and love what I do' attitude, and the knowing that you had touched others, made a difference, literally changed lives. Rekindled was my burning desire to empathize, encourage, and inspire hope to others — on paper and through my actions and attitude.

I wanted to briefly share with you excerpts from my notes and writing assignments as described in the workshop, your book, and from your website:

'The Cards' and 'Tom was right.'

4/28/02 2:30 a.m. — Notes from my first pack of 4" x 6" unlined index cards:

This seems overwhelming when I see how many blank cards are left...want to stop writing and go to sleep, yet want to complete my goal...don't know that I've really said anything yet but keep writing what comes to mind...almost seems out of my control. Finally, the last stack of cards from the first pack, but now I don't want to stop! Card #99 of the first stack! Have written a lot, but don't see any story developing yet, but that's what Tom said is supposed to happen.

Tom was right, writing on the cards is very helpful in self-examination and expression of private thoughts and fears...sure do ask myself a lot of questions, particularly, why?

4/30/02 — Still filled with a lot of emotions and questions — not a whole lot of detail about a story coming out yet, but that's what Tom predicted. He was right again, the more I write longhand, the better and easier it is to read and still write with speed. Last card in today's stack – time to try another of Tom's ideas – acknowledge my accomplishment and go stand in the waves and watch the pelicans again.

5/3/02 – I think doing cards is very helpful, but really want to start writing some kind of story. Tom said I would feel that way and he's on target again.

5/5/02 – Very protective of MY CARDS! Dorito chip on chair and seagull wanted it – don't care as long as he doesn't peck at my cards.

5/8/02 – When I ran out of things to say, ideas for Lowell's story started flowing. Hey, Tom, I think my 'AW' is finally getting a chance to speak. It feels great!

5/11/02 – Tom encouraged writing in the morning – not sure about that since I seem to be more nocturnal, but I do feel better and accomplished when writing first thing…get feelings out and no stress to finish them if tired or interrupted later…don't disappoint myself.

5/14/02 – My writing sabbatical – Four days, just me, myself, and I. Heaviest yet, most important thing I had to haul upstairs were 'my cards.' First thing I thought of to do when I woke up this morning was start writing – didn't matter what…just write. This is me – what feels comfortable and natural and of value – talking with my pen rather than my mouth.

5/15/02 – Just like Tom predicted, I'm not writing as many index cards – not as many emotions to deal with. Actually started work on draft of short story instead. Tom, I LOVE these cards – with my personality, I don't know how I lived without them. Have cards, have pens, will travel.

5/17/02 – Finished the drafts of 3 short stories – Tom was right (again) – this feels great! Must be feeling more confident with my writing because I'm asking *more people to read it. Am very open, even eager for all comments — anything to improve. I think Tom mentioned that, too.*

Helpful Hints to Avoid Panic:
I learned quickly that you need to stock your 'writing arsenal.' Minor panic set in when I only had 1/2 stack of cards left and so much to write! Furthermore, always have enough pens so if one runs out of ink, which happened more quickly than I ever would have expected, I have a back up so I can keep writing.

Another lesson I learned — Hold onto your cards when you stand up when sitting at the water's edge — luckily they floated in the salt water and dried without running or sticking together.

Success Story from Deborah Tyler Blais

From: Deborah Tyler Blais
To: Tom Bird
Author: *Letting Your Heart Sing*

My schedule is a little fuller than I anticipated, but I love it. After the book had been out about four months, the tide turned, and I no longer had to bang on doors, send e-mails, or make phone calls to book dates for book signings or talks. Word of mouth traveled fast, and people and organizations began vying for my time! Yesterday, I met Rosie O'Donnell and gave her a book (who knows where that may lead). And a member of one of my spiritual groups was a producer with the Oprah Show for seven years. He LOVES the book and is doing everything he can to help me get the book on Oprah.

I can hardly keep up with the correspondence from readers and keep getting asked, 'When is the Workbook coming out?' I am currently working on it and expect it will be out next year. I don't know how this happened, but *Letting Your Heart Sing* made its way into a women's prison, and they have started a Bliss Group there and are using the tools in my book to change their lives, so that when they get out, they do not have to return to a life of crime. Instead, they can live the lives they were always meant to. I can't tell you how much joy and gratitude that brings me.

So, Tom, in ways you can't even imagine, the work we did together continues to transform lives everywhere.

I refer people to your web site constantly, so don't think I'm not thinking about you, I am. And I can't thank you enough for helping me fulfill my deepest heart's desire: to share my stories in such a way as to inspire others to follow their heart's desires, so that they too can experience the indescribable joy that comes from letting their heart sing.

Law #2

A thorough understanding of the inner workings of the publishing industry is essential.

B Y ITS LITERAL, SIMPLE DEFINITION, PUBLISHING TRANSLATES to the preparing and then issuing of material for distribution and/or sale to the public.

However, to most authors it equates to much, much more. It represents recognition leading to personal and professional advancement, the expression of talent, passion, intelligence, respect, and to the penning of a record destined to live on through the ages.

As a result, there is nothing more influential in our culture than the written, and especially, published word. It is the foundation for everything we have been taught and entertained by. As a result, no art form-not acting, sculpting, or painting-garners more respect than writing. Is it any wonder then that 81% of Americans, in a survey recently quoted by *The New York Times*, said that they felt they had a book inside of them?

Yet, because of all the esteem lauded upon publishing and because those who teach it often have been so unsuccessful in approaching it themselves, an aura of impossibility has been draped around it.

I fully realize that there is a part of you, a self-sabotaging side, that is calling out for you to skip this section and instead launch yourself right into the nuts and bolts of getting published. But to do so would amount to literary suicide. The second biggest mistake that new writers make springs directly from not properly understanding their publishing options.

So, if getting published is sincerely your goal, read on.

Traditional Presses

There are three options, two of which I recommend, presently available for the publishing of books. I'll get into the publication of articles, short stories, and poetry later.

It is the traditional form of publishing, the first option we will examine, that we usually associate with the successful completion of this task. The traditional publishers no doubt do perform this task, but at what price to you, your career as an author, and to the potential of your work?

What a Book Publisher Does and Does Not Do, and How They Do It

Let's first define what it is that most believe these houses are responsible for doing. As I will show, they are not the all-knowing, all-caring, soon-to-make-you-successful publishing option that you may believe them to be.

Publish Your Book

The fact that they publish your book, making it available to the public, is absolutely correct.

Manage Your Cash Flow

A publisher is responsible for collecting all monies, accounting for it, and passing off your share of the profits to you.

Edit Your Book

Stories abound about how legendary authors stumbled upon the right editor, and it was that one editor who ended up being the primary driving force behind the success in that writer's career.

If you believe that option is still available to you, think again. The book publishing industry no longer has the monopoly on America's entertainment time that it once did. As a result, over the past few decades traditional publishing houses have resorted to publishing hundreds more books at a smaller profit margin just to keep up with cable, satellite television, videos, and other more convenient alternatives. The more books that a house is responsible for publishing, the more work that falls upon the shoulders of its editorial staff. However, most houses, in an attempt to keep down their overhead, have not increased the sizes of their editorial staffs to compensate for this shift. As a result, editors don't have the time they once had to transform you into a star.

In fact, it is you, as the author, who is responsible for making sure that your work has been edited before it is submitted.

Distribute Your Book

Traditional houses are indeed responsible for the distribution of your book. How well they complete this task, though, is up in the air. Will they simply hand it over to a nationally known distributor, will they utilize their own sales force as well, or in the best-case scenario, do both?

It is very important to have a crystal-clear understanding about the depth of commitment of a traditional house before signing on.

Market Your Book

Before we move into this topic, let me make it clear that marketing does not make a book into a bestseller. In fact, many a publisher has spent hundreds of thousands of dollars on a chosen book only to see the work land nowhere near a bestseller list.

Again, marketing does not make a book into a bestseller. It simply brings to the attention of a certain influential audience the release of the book. From that time forward, the book must stand on its own. It is word-of-mouth that is truly responsible for turning a book into a bestseller.

The vast majority of traditional publishers rely on an author to do his or her own marketing. To fool yourself into believing that once you sign on with a traditional publisher your house will promotionally take care of everything is delusional.

Even if a traditional publisher does decide to get involved with the promotion of your book, there is a more than an excellent chance that their tiny marketing and publicity staff can't handle your workload. Traditional publishing houses are also notoriously poor payers. Thus they don't attract the most proven promotional minds. So, even if they tried to promote your book, they probably could not follow through in a competent manner.

In fact, the marketing abilities of a traditional publisher are oftentimes so inadequate that even if a house does decide to promote an author's book, in most cases they have to employ the services of an outside firm to do it for them.

Design the Artwork for Your Book

Traditional publishers absorb the responsibility of the artwork associated with your book. But keep in mind that you will be using their artists and, thus, you may not have as much artistic control over how your product looks as you would like.

Copyright Your Book

Traditional publishers will copyright your book in your name and take the responsibility for performing other small legal tasks, including procuring the ISBN number. However, they will not take responsibility for offering you any sort of legal protection. In fact, as part of your contract, they may ask you to sign a waiver granting them immunity from any problems you may run into.

Represent the Specialty Rights for Your Book to Other Publishing Options

Part of a traditional publisher's role is to serve as a clearinghouse for the rights of your book. For example, a traditional publisher may purchase the hardback rights for your book. But the house may also serve as the agent to market your paperback rights to another house, as well as your serial rights, the reprinting of excerpts from your book in magazines and newspapers, and book club rights.

For their role in any transaction of this sort, they normally expect to receive a heafty percentage of all revenues generated.

Literary Agent Needed

Even though it is not an absolute must in every case, the vast majority of all traditional publishers, including all of the top houses, refuse to review any material written by a new writer who is not represented by a literary agent. This rule is in place to safeguard against a waste of time on their end by ensuring that you have the credibility necessary to justify their review. More on this is covered later. An agent's total take is normally 15% of your gross revenue, plus reimbursement of all his or her out-of-pocket expenses.

The Advance

Initially, if a traditional publisher is interested in your work, you will be offered an advance. I define an advance as "risk money applied against potential royalties earned."

Here's how it works. Let's say that you accept a $10,000 advance from a publisher, your book eventually sells for $20, and your 10% royalty rate is based on the cover price of the book. It can also be based on the net return received by the publisher. But, in that case, you would normally receive a much higher royalty rate to compensate for the discount afforded a bookstore or distributor. As it is, royalty rates range between 5%-25%. However, in the case above where your royalty rate was based on the cover price, you would receive $2 per book sold. In that case, then, how many books would your book need to sell to make back the advance you were offered? Correct: 5,000.

What would happen if your book sold only 3,000 copies? Would you then be responsible for returning

$4,000? Legally, you would be liable for the return of the unearned portion of the advance. However, if you have fulfilled your obligations as outlined under your contract with the publisher, rarely would you be expected to repay any part of your advance.

> *I just got a phone call from Llewellyn, and they want to publish my teen goddess book! Contract is in the mail. I am so happy I could fly!!!! Now I have to start writing my next book!*
>
> *Catherine Wishart, "Teenage Goddess: How to Look, Love, and Live Like a Goddess," (Llewellyn)*

The Amount of Money You Actually Receive

Let's use the scenario from above to sketch out how much money you would actually receive from the sale of your book.

Amount You Receive		Amount Your Publisher Receives	
Books Sold	60,000	Gross per Book	$ 12
Royalty	x $ 2	Production -	$ 3
	$120,000	Royalty -	$ 2
		Net per Book	$ 7
Agent's 15%	- 18,000		
Total	$102,000	Books Sold	60,000
		(@ 40% dis.) x	$ 7
			$420,000

For example, if your book sells the lofty total of 60,000 copies, you would receive $120,000, minus your agent's commission of 15%, for a total of $102,000. This, of course, does not include the monies generated by your publisher for outside sales to book clubs, paperback rights, etc.

How much is then pocketed by your publisher? In the case where your house sold 60,000 of your books on a straight 40% discount rate to stores, that would mean their gross revenue per book would end up being $12. However, after their production costs of $3 and the $2 they would have to pay you were subtracted, they would end up clearing $7 per book, or two or three times as much money as you were awarded for doing the bulk of the work by writing the book.

The 90-10 Reality

Please keep in mind that, especially in today's world, the vast majority of publishing houses are owned by corporations who care about nothing other than the bottom line. Thus, in essence, traditional publishers are nothing more or less than venture capitalists. They are willing to absorb a high risk on each of their dollars invested in exchange for a potential high return.

They are in the business to make money-period. They are not interested in influencing society or nurturing the career of a bright new writer, unless doing so would offer them a high return on their investment dollar.

You never expected justice from a company, did you?
They have neither a soul to lose nor a body to kick.

Sydney Smith

How much bottom-line revenue you and your book are worth, then, is their only consideration. What you and your book can generate for them is how they look at you. One of the ways that you can become more attractive to them is directly tied to what you will do to market your own book.

Publish and be damned.

Duke of Wellington

Yet, if you were under the misimpression that today's traditional publishers actually follow through on all of the tasks listed above, think again. Unless you have the good fortune of being one of their top 10% advances, do not expect them to put out any monies for the editorial work that might be needed on your book or for marketing it. You will be expected to deliver your manuscript to them in nearly perfect form. Plus, you will be responsible for doing all of the necessary promotion work and for paying for any advertisements, publicity, or for lining up talk show tours.

So important is your willingness to directly contribute in this area that a traditional publisher will actually expect you to state up front, before your book is considered for publication, how much you will be willing to offer marketing-wise toward the promotion of your own work. By limiting the monies they are expected to kick in, they also limit their liability. As a result, the $2 per book you could earn looks really small. This is especially the case if you decide to follow through on their suggestion to hire a professional publicity/marketing firm to promote your book. The rates for any of these firms usually range from $32,000-$45,000.

Amount You Receive	
Books Sold	60,000
Royalty	x $ 2
	$120,000
Agent's 15%	- 18,000
Total	$102,000
Promotion	- $40,000
	$ 62.000

So, for example, if you grossed the $102,000 via your 60,000-book sale stated earlier, and had to spend $40,000 promotionally, you would then have earned only $62,000, while your traditional publisher would have taken in $420,000:exactly the type of return a venture capitalist would expect.

Poverty is oftentimes associated with writing, but it is not because money is not being generated. It is only because so little of it is offered to the author, who has endured this type of misaligned business deal for centuries.

Credibility

Traditional publishers may rob you of your artistic, editorial, and literary freedom. They may offer you an insultingly low share of the profits, but a big-name, traditional publisher who lends you their good name offers you what no one else can — credibility. And it is credibility that most educated readers, who are also the best book buyers, relate to.

As a result of this credibility, more doors will be opened for you and your book personally, professionally, and literarily. The same credibility sets the foundation for sales. But, unfortunately, if you do not receive monies from a publisher to make you one of their top 10% properties, they won't promote your work.

Without promotion, the credibility is just that-credibility. However, no matter how applauded it is, without the necessary exposure of promotion, there is a superior chance that it will not translate into sales. And, if your book doesn't sell well, all credibility will be lost. So, it becomes a roll of the dice if you choose to go the traditional route.

Self-Publication

Former Drawbacks of Self-Publishing

Neale Donald Walsch, who wrote the bestselling *Conversations with God* series, literary legends Mark Twain, James Joyce, D. H. Lawrence, Stephen Crane, Edgar Allen Poe, Rudyard Kipling, Walt Whitman, George Bernard Shaw, Ezra Pound, Henry David Thoreau, Zane Gray, Carl Sandburg, and present-day literary legends John Grisham and James Redfield of the *Celestine Prophecy* connection: what two aspects do they all have in common?

First, their initial works all fell outside the lines of the ordinary, making them trendsetters. As a result, and secondly, they were left no alternative than to prove their worth by self-publishing.

Self-publishing is not the dregs to which the failed writer is left to retreat. Quite the contrary, it is the path of initiation for those trendsetters who oftentimes-like those mentioned above-go on to influence us the most. The publishing industry, being a hotbed of venture capitalists,is always and only looking for the safe and sure bet. Because their brilliance falls outside the ranks of the norm, trendsetters simply do not fit through the very narrow doorway of the traditional house.

Up until the last few years, though, no matter how popular an alternative it might have been for the trendsetter, self-publishing was littered with drawbacks.

Expensive

Until recently, the cost to produce a book was normally outside what an average American could spare or would want to spend. Just to have a manuscript typeset would often cost tens of thousands of dollars. Add into that the cost of a qualified style editor and you easily are in the $30,000 range. Then, in the past, to bring down the cost-per-unit price of one's book, high-quantity first runs of 10,000 copies or more were a necessity. So, the author would have no choice other than to sink at least another $40,000 into inventory, bringing his initial cash outlay to around $70,000.

Distribution

Even if one did self-publish, and somehow ended up with a saleable product, getting it in bookstores and distributed across the country was a whole new problem. In most cases, though, the future of a worthy book died on the dusty shelves in the author's garage or attic.

Less Than Worthy Alternatives

As the result of, and because of, an author's general lack of understanding and desperation, the door was oftentimes left wide open for the seemingly attractive vanity or subsidy presses to wield their evil wands. Their claims stated that they could supposedly do all that needed to be done better and at a price much lower than doing it on one's own. However, these presses, long the poisons of academics and vulnerable senior citizens, received the poor reputation they have for a reason.

Yes, they produced books, but these works were often poorly edited, poorly designed, and rarely ever promoted. As well, normally only enough copies were printed to soothe the author's fledgling ego. All of this was done, of course, so that the vanity or subsidy houses could keep as much of the fee charged to the author as possible. Sure, authors were often allowed as much as a 75% royalty rate, which was so attractive that their eyes bulged. However, no matter how you look at it, 75% of nothing is still nothing.

The extraordinary royalty rate was like the scent of blood to a hungry shark. Once the hopeful author was reeled in, the vanity or subsidy publisher would simply focus on getting the job done quickly and cheaply so as to keep as much of the fee charged to the writer as possible. To the vanity or subsidy house, promotion is too much work and the potential profit earned too slight to be considered even remotely attractive-especially when the next hungry sucker with the wide-open checkbook is usually waiting eagerly around the bend.

The Self-Publishing Solution

Though it may only have been by the sheer quality of their works and the Divine Guidance associated with them, the authors mentioned at the beginning of this section actually made it. However, the Divine, in today's market, has offered up a larger amount of assistance for those who choose to self-publish. That solution is referred to as Print On Demand presses or POD publishing.

It's like having a liscense to print your own money.

Lord Thomson of Fleet

As a result of the advent of the computer age, much has changed in the publishing industry in the last few years. The cost of typesetting a book, now commonly referred to as formatting, has dropped from tens of thousands of dollars to around the $1,500 range. The computer age has also enabled books to be stored in the memory of a computer and to be summoned at any time-the best time being when someone is ready and willing to purchase it. Thus evolved the name for this type of publishing alternative. Because of the computer age, a book can literally be called forward from memory and generated at the request of a buyer or potential purchaser. As a result, no major inventory has to be purchased by the author, eliminating costly expense number two, and the cost to publish a book dropped from $70,000 to around $2,000-$3,000.

Most POD presses also offer you a turnaround time (from receiving your manuscript and transforming it into a fully published book) of less than 30 days. Traditional presses take on average of between 9-13 months to perform the same task.

Add to that the fact that the most influential wholesale distributor of books in the world, Ingram, through its offshoot Lightning Source, has spearheaded this jolt to the industry by opening its own POD press (www.lightning-source.com for more information). So, Lightning Source will place your formatted book on their computer system, print however many copies are necessary, and send them out whenever there is an order. They will also collect the money paid for your book(s) and send it to you, and they offer international distribution as well. In fact, when you sign up with Lightning Source, there is practically nowhere of affluence on the planet that your book will not be available for purchase. So, Lightning Source will offer you many of the essential luxuries of a traditional press without having to give up 85-90% of your profit.

What a POD Press Does Offer

Just to keep straight all the information you have been exposed to so far, a legitimate POD press, such as Lightning Source, collects the money from purchases of your book and passes it along to you. So, they manage your cash flow. They also store your manuscript in their computer, print and publish it at a 'per book' price to you, and distribute it, making it available to individuals and bookstores all across the globe.

What a POD Press Does Not Offer

In essence, with a worthy POD house you will be serving as your own publisher. So, you will need to form a specific business entity to do so and give it a name. This can normally be accomplished for between $10-$100, depending upon the state in which you live.

As a result of accepting the reins of being your own publisher, the POD press becomes your printing house with distributing capabilities. This, of course, is what self-publishing houses, such as vanity or subsidy presses, have always been. However, in the past, these cagey creatures have been able to pass themselves off as more and thus, wound up charging more than they were worth. Thus the POD route is not only fast, efficient, and inexpensive, but is the most honest and forthright business deal yet offered the literary author/entrepreneur.

Again, what the POD press does do is print, distribute your book, and manage your cash flow for you. These services come at the cost of a modest, up-front fee of approximately $100 and the price it costs to print your

What They Do and Don't Do For You

Traditional Publisher
(for those not in the top 10%)

- Publish Your Book
- Manage Your Cash Flow
- Little or No Editing
- Offer Wide Distribution
- Little or No Marketing
- Artwork Designed by Staff *(little or no input from you)*
- Procure Copyright and ISBN
- Limited Legal Protection
- Represent Specialty Rights
- Require Literary Agent
- Offer Advance of Royalties
- Offer Reader Credibility
- Keep 85-90% of Profits

Print on Demand Presses

- You Pay to Publish the Book
- Manage Your Cash Flow
- Offers Wide Distribution
- You Control Marketing
- You Hire an Editor
- You Choose the Book Designer and Layout
- Art Designed by Your Artist
- You Obtain Copyright and ISBN
- You Manage Specialty Rights
- No Literary Agent Necessary
- No Advance of Royalties
- No Credibility
- You Retain 100% of Profit

book, which is in the range of $4 per paperback book and $8-10 for hardcover. This price is approximately 25% higher per book than you would expect to pay if you employed the past form of self-publishing. This is where a POD house makes its profit. However, if you go the POD route, you will also avoid the purchase and cost of carrying a big inventory.

What the POD house does not do is edit your book, take responsibility for the artwork, promote your book to other houses for the sale of other rights, or sell directly to the public. That is left up to you. But, again, outside the design of your work, traditional publishers would expect you to take care of all the editorial content and promote it as well. Also, you would hand over to them between 85-90% of your profit, while with a POD house you keep 100% of the gross.

When I attended a local writing class back in the middle 1990s, I discovered my passion; however, it wasn't until I began attending Tom Bird's classes that I learned how to 'dish up the soup from stove to table.' Through his various seminars, Tom has guided me from having words scribbled in longhand on yellow legal pads to professionally printed books I promote over regional television stations and at nationally known bookstores. Although few writers attain the level of success as McCarthy or Rawlings, we all must start somewhere, and with Tom's guidance, you gain a solid foundation on which to build.

Nancy Melinda Hunley, Knoxville, Tennessee, author of This Time Around, Love In the Middle Ages, and Southern Graces, An Incompleat Manual for Genteel Feminine Deportment, (L. A. Dydds)

What Does It Cost to Go POD?

The following options vary greatly in cost. In reality, you can self-publish your POD book for as little as a few hundred dollars if you choose to do the vast majority of the labor yourself.

I had one student go this route with her novel. However, despite the depth of her idea, her drive, and her passionate prose, the book looked like she had handled all of the tasks herself, and its dire need for editing took much away from the eventual success of the story. So, I wouldn't recommend going this route. Even though this student was able to clear her bottom line quickly, I strongly feel that her work lived a life far less than its potential. However, what you choose to do with the following is completely up to you. Just make sure you can live with your choices while offering your literary baby the chance it deserves.

Formatting

Formatting translates to converting your manuscript into the design of a book. The person you hire for this task is by far the most important individual you will deal with. No matter how much work you put into your book, if you try to skimp here to save a few bucks, and the formatter you hire does a less-than-adequate job, your book will look terrible. As a result, your book sales will wane, if not disappear altogether.

Make sure as well that your formatter has worked with the POD press you choose. If he or she has not, you may wind up paying for this person's education to learn how to do so.

Ask to see examples of this person's work, and don't be shy about requesting a list of professional references. Let your potential formatters read some of your manuscript before signing on. Not only will this give you an idea of how sincere the person is, but doing so will also allow you to audit and compare any ideas they may have for formatting your book. This person needs to be not only technically sound and proven, but creative and artistic as well.

Good formatters are hard to find, so start searching for this person as soon as possible.

To find competent formatters, you can check out my website, **www.TomBird.com**, or contact the POD press that you are most interested in, or call printers in your area for recommendations. Some PODs will even provide this service for you. Get potential formatters to quote you a flat fee, which is the best way to prevent any hidden costs and foul-ups on their end that could end up costing you more than you planned. Depending upon the length of your book and the style in which you will want it formatted, this option would cost you between $600-$1800. If that sounds like a lot of money to you, please keep in mind how important the presentation of your book is, as well as the fact that only a few years ago this service, via typesetting, would have cost you tens of thousands of dollars.

Cover Design

Again, like the student mentioned previously, you can do this yourself. However, there is a good chance that your potential readers will be able to tell. In that case, you may lose book sales. The first thing that a potential reader sees is the cover of your book. If it looks unprofessional or does not grab his or her attention, you lose a sale.

As with formatters, a good cover artist is hard to find. A cover artist needs to be creative, so don't be afraid to ask for a review of their ideas on your book cover before entering into any type of agreement. Ask for professional references and examples of previous covers. Make sure, too, that he or she is intimately familiar with meeting the demands of your POD house. Otherwise, you may end up paying for the education this person should already possess.

Avoid, at all costs, web services whose prices seem cheaper than others but offer only a few stock styles of cover for you to choose from. It is best and most professional-looking if you have something individually created for your cover.

As with formatters, start looking for this person early and get candidates to quote you a flat rate. Average costs for this service range from $600-$900. Potential recommendations for cover artists can be found from the same sources as formatters.

Editing

Even if you were one of those few young adults or children who somehow picked up the force-feeding of grammar, punctuation, and spelling while in school, at some point you will become blind to a credible review of your own work. So, it is essential that you have your book copyedited by someone else-hopefully a professional-before handing it over to your formatter.

The *Literary Market Place* (LMP), which is available in any good library, is highly recommended as a source for copyeditors. A reasonable cost for copyediting a book is $2 per page.

There is also a second type and potentially more important brand of this work that needs to be taken into consideration as well, and that is style-editing.

You need to have your book style-edited if you have not done everything necessary to properly compose your work. To avoid this potentially large and unnecessary expense, I strongly suggest applying the step-by-step method shared in my book *You Were Born to. . . Write*.

However, if you already have a manuscript fully completed or if after employing the methods in *You Were Born to. . . Write* you still feel you need the services of a style editor, listings of sources can be found in the *Literary Market Place* (LMP-available in all libraries) or through recommendations made on my website.

Make sure when interviewing potential candidates for this position that you request the usual references and examples of work. Let your candidates also review a sampling of your work to see what suggestions they may have for improvement.

As you go over your candidates' suggestions for improvement, pay very special attention to their objectivity. You want to ensure that you will be working with an objective editor and not a frustrated writer. In the case of the latter, this person will attempt to rewrite your book for you in his or her style, as opposed to trying to aid you in bringing out your own voice. Prices for a competent style editor range from $800-$10,000.

Legal

As mentioned, you will need to form your own business entity to go the POD route, which can range anywhere in cost from $10-$100. I would also suggest that you at least run your chosen arrangement by a competent accountant or attorney. I routinely budget $250, which is normally more than enough to cover the cost of the review.

You will also be responsible for the copyrighting of your material. When choosing your POD house, check into what services they offer. Do they handle the copy-right of your material or do you?

If you are responsible for your own, you can complete the task online for approximately $35 through the Library of Congress. Your attorney can also handle it. With an attorney's fee included, it would cost several hundred dollars more than the $35 charged if you go directly through the Library of Congress.

If you would like an attorney to review your manu-script for any potential legally dangerous statements or claims, a service normally provided by traditional houses, there are plenty of lawyers qualified to do so. They can be found under the title of Intellectual Property Attorneys.

However, when you boil it all down, all that is legally necessary for you to do is start your own company. As mentioned, the costs for this service run between $10-$100, but it is suggested that you budget $250 just in case you choose to seek the advice of a professional. Thus, unless you decide it's worth the thousands of dollars it would take to obtain an attorney to review your manu-script, I suggest that budgeting $250 would be more than sufficient.

Promotion

Once, at an Intensive Retreat I was offering in my home in Sedona, Arizona, Dick O'Connor, a longtime New York editor I had brought in to co-present, made a very inter-esting point.

In trying to illustrate where it was that our students should focus their promotional attention as authors, he drew a small dot in the middle of a flip chart.

"What is this?" he asked.

After no one replied, Dick answered for them. "The number of Americans who read hardback books."

Then he drew a small circle around the dot and asked, "What's this?"

Again, no one dared to answer, so he replied for them a second time. "The number of people who read paperback books."

Then Dick drew a huge circle around the smaller circle, and asked for a third time, "What's this?"

No longer waiting for a response, Dick replied quickly this time to his own query. "Those who don't read books."

I have read numerous books on writing, publishing, and selling creative works from authors such as William Goldman, David Trottier, Skip Press, and the list goes on. While the information from these experts has been invaluable, I would put Tom Bird's unique voice right up at the top of the heap.
Debbie D., student, U.S.A.

The point I'm trying to make here is that expensive, major media blanket advertising is a waste of time for authors. There is a small, enthusiastic audience that needs to be approached. After that has been successfully completed, you can do as any other publisher would: rely on word-of-mouth to sell your book for you.

If you are writing fiction, the best way to do this is through reviews written on your book. The three most influential reviewers in the industry, because they cater mostly to the large-scale purchasers of books, are *Publishers Weekly*, *Kirkus Reviews*, and *The Library Journal*. Each of these publications has sites on the Internet that will tell you exactly what needs to be done to have your book considered for a review. Keep in mind, though, that with these three reviewers, or any others, it is in your best interest to get your book, even if it is in rough form, into their hands as far in advance of your planned publication date as possible.

As far as other magazines, syndication services, and newspapers are concerned, the corporate names and addresses can be found in the *Literary Market Place* (LMP) which is usually available at libraries.

As far as costs for promoting your fiction is concerned, you need to set aside enough cash to cover the expenses of review copies and their mailing costs. Besides that, you will need a website.

Now, I know that it is possible to set up a website for under $50. The trouble with that site though is that it looks like a website that you set up for under $50. Because so much of the world is cyber-attuned, it is important to have a nice site.

Scan the Internet for the websites of some of your favorite authors and take notes of what they have done. Then use either an Internet service or personal references to help you access lists of site designers. Follow the same procedures that you employed when acquiring the services of your editor, artist, or formatter. Ask for references and for them to offer you ideas on what they would do with your site. Ask for examples of their work as well. Accept only a flat, all-inclusive price as their bid to enable you to avoid the mystery and disappointment of the hourly rate. Also, make sure your webmaster has the abilities to upload your materials on your book to major bookselling sites such as Amazon.com and BarnesandNoble.com, and to attune your website to the liking of search engines, which will eventually lead to your popularity on the Internet.

Including the reservation of your website name, yearly fees, and your programmer's labor, I would budget $1,200.

Regarding non-fiction, beyond the use of reviews and a well-done website to stimulate interest in your book, radio and television interviews are also a large asset. The finest route to gain access to every TV and radio interviewer in the country is through a publication titled *Radio-Television Interview Reporter* (RTIR).

RTIR sports listings and descriptions of books and their authors and is sent out three times a month to every major and minor media source in the country. Over 21,000 media are contacted with each mailing.

RTIR usually offers a collection of specials, all ranging in the area of $1,200 per six-ad contract, which covers not only the running of six of your ads, but an array of other services and products as well, including a database of their entire media mailing list.

I highly recommend the use of this service. Like most good businesses, RTIR has an extensive website that can answer all of your questions.

Lastly, to best understand all of the promotional opportunities available to you, I strongly suggest reading Rick Frishman's books *Guerrilla Publicity: Hundreds of Sure-Fire Tactics to Get Maximum Sales for Minimum Dollars* and *Guerrilla Marketing for Writers : 100 Weapons to Help You Sell Your Work*.

Rick is the president of the largest and most influential book publicity firm in the world, Planned Television Arts (or PTA), and he is a marketing genius. Even though each of his two books costs only $14.95, they are worth their weight in gold.

Read both books, take notes if you like, and then start playing with the valuable suggestions Rick makes. Choose what feels comfortable to you, leave the rest behind, and then keep promoting.

PTA also works out a special deal for my students as long as you are willing to do the majority of the legwork. If you would like their direct assistance in promoting your book, they will design a professional promotional campaign for you and implement it over half a year for an average of $1,500 per month. Even though this may sound expensive, the services and instructions you will receive are comparable to what some traditional publishers pay 3-4 times as much for. The big difference is that you wind up doing the majority of the legwork, but the price is a very good investment, especially if a full-time author is what you want to be.

Credibility

While a traditional publisher oftentimes offers credibility, the POD press, especially since you will be publishing under the name of your own house, cannot help you in that area.

However, book sales equate to reputations and good reputations equate to credibility. So, the better job you do, the more book sales you will gain, and the more credibility you will be building for your house.

Hardly anyone had heard of tiny Hampton Roads Press until they published Walsh's *Conversations with God*, which was eventually sold to a major house who made it into a bestseller. Now, everyone in the publishing world knows of Hampton Roads as one of the finest New Age publishers in the business. All it takes is one big book.

Choosing the Right POD House

Even though the POD industry is relatively new, it hasn't taken long for some unworthy alternatives to infiltrate the most innovative, author-friendly step forward in the history of publishing. Since there is no inner governing body of ethics in this industry to keep snakes from creeping in, it is up to you, the author and the most important spoke in the publishing wheel, to discern for yourself who is right and wrong for you.

Your decision should boil down to a few basic facts:

1. Turnaround Time: How quickly will the POD house be able to produce your book? Don't settle for anything over 30 working days.

2. Background: Ask for references and samples of books they have published. Time in business is also an important factor.

3. Cost: How much do they charge and especially what is it that you can expect for your fee?

4. Print Cost: How much will it cost to have your book printed, and how quickly can they promise to get orders out for you?

5. Royalties: A true POD house doesn't pay royalties to their authors because the authors are given 100% of all monies received. Now there are those houses that refer to themselves as PODs but proudly proclaim they pay their authors a whopping 25% royalty rate. Let me straighten this out for you. You pay for all the expenses to have your book edited and printed, and they don't provide any type of service at all in these cases. You write the book and then you pay them to simply add it to their computer database. Then they profit from every book you have printed and they want to receive 75% of the monies from the sale of the book? For doing what? May those with eyes actually see the truth behind such a scandal. In fact, may even those without eyes see it.

POD Costs	
Expenditures	**Low/High Budget**
Formatting	$0 / $1,800
Cover Design	$600 / $1200
Copyediting *(based on a 300-page book)*	$0 / $600
Style Editing	$0 / $2,500
Legal	$0 / $250
Promotion Review Copies *(250 copies @ $5 each plus* *$3 each mailing)*	$0 / $2,000
RTIR Ad	$0 / $1,200
POD Publisher	$100 / $600
Professional Publicist	$0 / $9,000
TOTALS:	$700 / $19,150

You can tailor your POD publishing plan to your taste and budget. However, to make your decision easier for you, I decided to plot the two extremes for you. Like most of my students, you will probably end up spending a total somewhere in the middle.

6. Credibility: At this juncture in their development, a POD press does not offer you any credibility. If someone from a POD house tells you that your association with their name does offer you credibility, run-don't walk-away from them.

Distribution

Ingram is the finest, most accepted, and best-known wholesale distributor of books in the world. If a POD house that you are considering does not use them, you should ask why. No other distributor of books even comes close to matching up.

What I suggest doing is rating each POD press in each of the categories listed above from 1-10, with 10 being the highest rating. Then, since the topic of royalties and distribution are the two most important categories for the long-term, double whatever the score each POD alternative comes up with in those two areas. Then add up your totals. The highest score should be the right POD house for you.

Articles, Short Stories, and Poetry

Contrary to what you may have been told, articles, short stories, and poetry are not the best door to go through to become the published author of books you may want to be. In fact, quite the opposite is true. If you want to write articles, short stories, and poetry, the most successful way to do so is to first become a known commodity as a successful author of books.

Even though I have included in this book information on this alternative, I simply do not recommend it as a quick, painless, and direct route to authoring books.

The Ultimate of All Solutions

Let's keep in mind that whatever it is that you have coming through to write, or which has already come through you and has been written, is like your literary child, and as with a child of any sort, you want the best for it. How you offer this child to the public is where publishing comes in.

Forget about all the prestige, wealth, and fame that you may have inappropriately associated with publishing. All publishing is really there to do is make available to the public whatever literary gift you may have. That's it.

When looking at it from that perspective, choosing the right publishing option is really not much different than picking the right college or university to further a child's education and training.

Beyond all the financial drawbacks and the loss of artistic, editorial, and literary control, the traditional publishers, because of the credibility associated with them and the massive influence and money they can put behind you if you end up being in their top 10% books, are still the best option. Thus I suggest that you wholeheartedly pursue that option first. How to do just that is what the majority of the remainder of this book is devoted to showing you.

After you have played out that option and if you do not land a contract as one of a publisher's top 10% books, then go the POD route, which will teach you more about the world of publishing than you ever thought possible.

Once you've used POD to sell a few thousand copies of your book, proving that there is indeed a market for it, re-approach the world of traditional publishing if you like, or stay with POD. Either way, your valuable literary child will have found its way into the world — which is simply what publishing is there to provide and nothing more.

❧

To help you understand what needs to be performed if going the POD route and when, I have included [in Appendix A] a slightly modified checklist as designed by one of my students, Shirley Hildreth of Muse Imagery in Las Vegas, Nevada. Shirley has become so successful at organizing this system that she has now begun working with new authors in leading them through this process.

At the conclusion of Shirley's checklist, I have also included some sample announcements and review response forms also utilized by Shirley.

I attended one of Tom's seminars due to a phone call from a friend. They saw an ad in the local paper and thought I might be interested. I thought I was going to learn about publishing, but I learned so much more. I was in the middle of writing my first book. To my amazement, Tom described what I had been experiencing. Listening to Tom not only validated my experience, but gave me the confidence to let the process flow more freely. Tom's methods and inspiration will guide you to allow your creative spirit to be released. The words will flow freely, and the experience will be fulfilling beyond what you can imagine. The book will write itself! Tom's books will guide you from start to finish — writing through publishing.

Mary McGovern, Paulden, Arizona, author of The Reason We Are Here — The Truth, (Veravail)

Law #3

**If you are so led, collaborating on a
book with a well-known source or celebrity
is a great way to get published fast.**

I HAVE INCLUDED THIS CHAPTER BECAUSE IT DETAILS POSSIBLY the most safe, secure, and profitable arena for a new writer to break into the publishing field. If you are drawn in this direction, I strongly recommend that you pursue this option.

Within this specific field, a writer can choose one of two routes to follow. The first route is that of being a ghostwriter. The second path is that of a co-author. Though the two may sound similar to the novice or non-writer, they are vastly different in structure, design, output, credit, and pay.

Ghostwriting

By definition, ghostwriters are simply glorified secretaries. That doesn't mean that they are without talent. It just means that they are called upon to use fewer of their abilities than a co-author.

A ghostwriter is usually called in when a celebrity or expert in one field or another has some prepared material, no matter how rough it may be, and is asked to reform it, retype, and edit this gobbledygook into shape. The ghostwriter is usually paid a one-time fee.

And even though a good ghostwriter can oftentimes build up a substantial reputation for himself or herself among his or her peers or among editors in the business, they receive either no, or at best very little, credit for their work. Rarely are their names listed alongside that of the celebrity on the cover of the book, they usually don't receive any cut of the royalties, and they are usually given no real credit for any of the success the book eventually experiences.

Co-Authoring

A co-author actually authors any book they are involved with. As a result, they receive an ample amount of credit and are paid a vast amount more than a ghostwriter. Their names are printed alongside that of the celebrity on the cover of the book. They are usually paid a percentage of all revenues generated by the book, and share the copyright with their co-author.

All in all, if you can get it, co-authoring is the best way to go. But don't allow anyone, especially someone who has never done it before, convince you that it is easy to co-author. To be able to unselfishly capture the voice, tone, and message of your celebrity, you have to give up your own views and biases, incessantly research your subject, and probe the psyche of your celebrity for the truth behind his or her innermost thoughts and feelings. Again, it takes a unique person to be able to do this, and editors know that. But the residuals, and the pay, are much better than ghostwriting, if you can make the unselfish adjustments.

At the end of this section is a copy of a standard collaborative agreement that I have been using for nearly ten years. Since everything is negotiable in this type of dealing, I simply keep this contract on file in my computer and adjust it to meet each particular situation. If you are interested in entering the field of co-authoring, I suggest that you do the same thing.

All the specific points and paragraphs in the sample collaborative agreement located at the end of this chapter are essential. But since I feel that the majority of the elements in the agreement are self-explanatory, I will only highlight the major points. Each major point and where it can be found in the sample contract are listed as well.

Duties and Restrictions: Paragraphs 2, 6, & 11

In any collaborative agreement, it is essential to specifically spell out what each party will be responsible for doing. As a writer, it is also important to make it clear that you will be working on other projects besides the one mentioned in the contract. As far as your celebrity's duties are concerned, make sure he or she commits to reviewing all your work and all proofs in a timely fashion. Getting a celebrity to commit to a major promotional role shortly after the book is released is also in your best career and financial interests.

Title of the Work: Paragraph 3

Co-authors need to share in all major decisions. Thus it is important that both co-authors have a say in the eventual title of the book. Though if it comes down to whether you get the credit of your name on the book's cover or an equal say in what the eventual title will be, go for the listing of your name.

Approval by Celebrity: Paragraph 4

It is extremely important that your celebrity approve anything that you write in his or her voice. That way the celebrity will have to take responsibility for what is said through you, and you will be protected from becoming a scapegoat, if what it said isn't received as well as he or she expected it to be.

Preservation of the Celebrity's Rights: Paragraph 5

For the sake of being fair, it is only right that you pledge, as a worthy co-author, not to reveal any secrets or information to outside parties that may be considered private and personal to your celebrity.

Ownership of Copyright: Paragraph 9

This is always a major negotiation point, because whoever owns the copyright owns the book. Thus, the owner of the copyright can call the shots on what is done with it.

Income: Paragraph 10

As a co-author, your biggest concern should always be covering your time and expenses to write a book. So you want to acquire the highest percentage of upfront money possible. The best you can usually hope for when working with a national celebrity is 50%. But, of course, all of this is dependent upon the potential amount of money a project may bring in. Receiving a decent percentage of the total royalty revenue after the upfront money should be viewed as a bonus.

Arbitration: Paragraph 14

Utilizing any other route besides arbitration to dispute a difference between co-authors can take years in court and cost tens of thousands of dollars. Thus it is best for all concerned if you and your co-author agree to settle any disputes between yourselves in arbitration as opposed to an open court setting.

Death and Disability: Paragraphs 15 & 16

It will be in your best interests if, in the event of the unfortunate death or disability of your co-author, you retain the rights to complete the collaboration. As well, it is in the best interest of your estate that they retain the rights to have the collaborative work completed in your absence if something should happen to you.

Literary Agent: Paragraph 18

Since you will be the most qualified source in this regard, it is always best if you can choose the right literary agent for the both of you, with the proper consent of your co-author, of course.

Governing Law: Paragraph 21

Since the hiring of out-of-town legal counsel can not only be a major inconvenience but very expensive, the locale in which any disputes between you and your co-author are tried is an important issue.

Sample Collaboration Agreement

COLLABORATION AGREEMENT

AGREEMENT made as of the _____ day of _____, 20____, by and between _____ (hereinafter called "_____") and TOM BIRD of Pittsburgh, Pennsylvania, (hereinafter called "BIRD"):

WHEREAS, the parties desire to collaborate on a project currently untitled, the content of which they agree will concern the views, playing days, coaching days, and life of _____ (hereinafter called the "Work") and to provide for the sale, lease, license, and other disposition of the rights thereto;

NOW, THEREFORE, in consideration of the premise and of the mutual promises and undertakings herein contained, and for other good and valuable consideration, receipt and sufficiency of which is hereby acknowledged, the parties agree as follows:

1. Collaboration. The parties shall make themselves available to each other at times and places mutually agreeable to discuss the Work. They shall collaborate exclusively with each other in, and perform the services necessary for, the preparation and writing of the Work and the publication and promotion of the Work.

2. Duties and Restrictions.
   a. _____ shall cooperate with BIRD in the preparation of an outline of the Work, in the

preparation of the entire Work, and in the correction of all proofs of the Work.

b. BIRD shall be solely responsible for writing the book-length manuscript and for obtaining any and all necessary permissions for use of copyrighted or other proprietary material. BIRD shall prepare and deliver the manuscript of the Work to _____ for _____ approval within a sufficient time to allow _____ to review the Work and to allow BIRD to make any necessary revisions before the manuscript delivery date stipulated in _____ and BIRD's contract with the book publisher. _____ shall revise the text, if necessary, pursuant to _____ recommendations. BIRD and _____ agree to revise the manuscript according to the publisher's reasonable recommendations, if any. BIRD shall deliver the text of the Work to the book publisher in accordance with the publishing schedule, as that may be adjusted or extended from time to time.

c. The parties agree that both of them will be involved in the negotiation of any contract(s) for publication or for any other exploitation of the Work, that both will be listed as authors on any such contract(s), and that both will execute any such contracts.

3. Title of the Work. The title of the Work in all forms in English throughout the world shall be subject to the express approval of _____ and BIRD.

4. Approval by. Any information concerning the events, persons, facts, circumstances, or stories of his life and career that _____, in his sole judgment, deems confidential shall at all times be treated as such and respected by BIRD. This provision shall survive the termination or expiration of this Agreement.

5. Preservation of Rights. All rights of _____, including rights in his life material, personal performance, and personal appearance rights, or rights to use, reproduce, or represent his likeness, face, voice, name, or body, in whole or in part, for purposes of personal appearance in film or on stage, endorsements, advertisements, or charitable or educational appearances, or otherwise are reserved by _____, except as are reasonably necessary for the purposes of this Agreement.

6. BIRD's Duties and Restrictions. _____ acknowledges that BIRD will be engaged in other pursuits during the time he is performing under this Agreement, which pursuits are likely to include authorship of other books, articles, and literary compositions, and that BIRD will not devote his entire time to the purposes of this Agreement. BIRD agrees, however, to diligently apply himself hereunder and to render his best efforts to the purposes of this Agreement. BIRD hereby agrees that he will not, without written permission of _____, publish, authorize, assist in or associate himself editorially or in any other manner with the publication or production, in any form whatsoever, of material based on or incorporating any portion of the events, persons, facts, circumstances, stories,

or other material concerning _____ life and career. This provision shall survive the termination and expiration of this Agreement.

7. Joint Venture. The parties hereby form a joint venture. The parties do not intend by this Agreement to form a partnership between them, nor shall this Agreement be construed to constitute a partnership.

8. Joint Work. The parties intend that their contributions to the Work be merged into inseparable or interdependent parts of a unitary whole, so that the Work shall be a joint work under Art. 101 of the Copyright Act of 1976 of which the parties shall be co-authors.

9. Ownership of Copyright. _____ and BIRD shall be joint owners of the copyright in the Work during its initial and any renewal or extended terms, in all forms and all languages throughout the world, and all material prepared in connection with the Work and any registration of copyright in the Work shall be in the names of both _____ and BIRD.

10. Income. All income accruing from any exploitation of the Work, including any contract with a publisher, shall be divided equally between the parties, up through and including the first $50,000 received from any publisher or other licensee; thereafter, income will be divided at the rate of sixty percent (60%) to _____ and forty percent (40%) to BIRD. All contracts relating to exploitation of the

Work shall specify said division of royalties as well as require statements from the payor to each party.

11. Review of Manuscript and Galleys. The parties agree each will promptly review the copyedited manuscript and galleys.

12. Indemnity. The parties agree to share equally the authors' responsibilities of warranty and indemnity as expressed in any contract for the exploitation of the Work, including those for reasonable attorneys' fees, except that in any instance where any breach is the result of negligence of one of the parties (including failure to obtain permissions or other unauthorized use of copyrighted material), then such party will be solely responsible for any costs or damages incurred by the Publisher or any licensee of the Work and by the non-responsible party.

13. Consent for Reuse of Materials. The parties agree that neither will incorporate material based on or derived from the Work in any subsequent work without the consent of the other.

14. Arbitration. Any controversy or claim arising out of or relating to this agreement or any breach thereof shall be settled by arbitration in accordance with the Rules of the American Arbitration Association of the City of Philadelphia, and award rendered by said arbitrators shall be treated as a final and non-appealable judgment of any court having jurisdiction thereof. The preceding sentence shall not apply to disputes concerning the editorial content of the Work.

15. Death or Disability Before Completion of the Manuscript. The death or disability of either _____ or BIRD prior to the completion of the manuscript of the Work shall not terminate this Agreement unless the Work shall become commercially unsaleable thereby. In the event of the death or total disability of BIRD, his personal repre sentatives shall secure, at the expense of BIRD or his estate, a substitute author, acceptable to _____ and to the book publisher, to complete the Work, and BIRD or his estate shall continue to be entitled to all the benefits of this Agreement. In the event BIRD or his estate does not obtain a substitute author acceptable to _____, _____ shall have the right to retain the services of a substitute author of his own choice. In that event, the reasonable compensation to such substitute author for completing the Work shall be deducted from BIRD's share of the income accruing from the exploitation of the Work, and _____, in his sole discretion, shall determine what copyright interest, if any, the substitute author shall receive. In the event of the total disability of _____, _____ shall make his best efforts to provide life materials to BIRD and to accomplish the purposes of this Agreement. In the event of the death of _____, this Agreement will terminate, unless, in the judgment of BIRD and the book publisher, sufficient life materials have been made or can be made available to BIRD so that he can complete the Work, and the Work will be commercially saleable, in which case BIRD may elect to continue this Agreement, and the Agreement shall be binding upon heirs and estates.

16. Death of_____ or BIRD After Completion of the Manuscript. If, after the completion of the Manuscript, BIRD dies, _____ shall have the right alone to negotiate and contract for the publication and other exploitation of the Work; make revisions in any subsequent editions; and generally act with regard thereto as if he were the sole author, except that _____ shall cause BIRD's share of the proceeds as provided in this Agreement to be paid to his estate, and shall furnish to his estate copies of all contracts made by _____ pertaining to the Work. If, after completion of the manuscript, _____ dies, BIRD shall have the right and the obligation to negotiate and contract for the publication and exploitation of rights in the Work, subject to the approval of _____ estate, and he shall cause _____ share of the proceeds as provided in this Agreement to be paid to _____ estate, and shall furnish to _____ estate copies of all contracts pertaining to the Work.

17. Term. This Agreement, unless otherwise terminated under the terms hereof, shall continue for the life of any copyright in the Work and any and all renewals or extensions of said copyright.

18. Literary Agent. Unless otherwise agreed in writing, BIRD will also serve as the exclusive selling agent of the Work, and is expected to diligently and faithfully use all reasonable efforts to effectuate the sale, lease, license, or transfer of rights to the Work.

19. Waiver. Failure on the part of any party to insist upon strict compliance by the other with any term, covenant, or condition hereof shall not be deemed to be a waiver of such term, covenant, or condition.

20. Benefit. This Agreement shall inure to the benefit of, and shall be binding upon, the executors, administrators, heirs, and assigns of the parties.

21. Entire Understanding and Governing Law. This Agreement constitutes the entire understanding of the parties, may be amended or modified only in writing signed by the parties, and shall be governed by the laws of the Commonwealth of Pennsylvania.

22. Counterparts. This Agreement may be signed in two or more counterparts, each of which shall be an original for all purposes.

IN WITNESS WHEREOF, the parties hereunto have set their respective hands and seals as of the day and year first above written.

WITNESS: COLLABORATORS

_____   _____

_____   _____
                                   Tom Bird

Success Story from Paul L. Hall

From: Paul L. Hall, Troy, Michigan
To: Tom Bird
Author: *Our Father, The Big Island* and *Places the Dead Call Home*

I think of myself primarily as a novelist, a writer of fiction. But I've long since acknowledged that the likelihood of my making a living solely by writing fiction is, well, statistically slim. Not that I intend to stop writing fiction. It's just that I need to support myself in the meantime.

With the expanded opportunities for publishing that have emerged over the past few years, establishing one's expertise and credentials with a book—especially a nonfiction book—has opened a new and lucrative field for writers such as myself. I have been a public relations practitioner for more than 25 years, a discipline that requires me to effectively communicate my clients' unique "stories" to various audiences, including the media. The other part of the job is convincing the media, ideally based on the pure news value of the story itself, to publicize my clients' products and/or services. More and more of my clients are recognizing that writing a book provides a means of achieving both these communications and publicity objectives in a relatively efficient way. I say "relatively efficient" because, for a variety of reasons, most of these clients would rather publish a book than write one.

It's not because they aren't smart, motivated, or industrious enough to write the book. Usually it's a matter of not having the time or the experience (which, of course, requires time in accumulating). In other cases, they lack confidence in their writing abilities. For whatever reason, they turn to co-authors (or ghost-writers) like me to help them with the job.

This has provided a welcome stream of income for me, but it has also provided other benefits. First, I am always learning something new, whether it's about event marketing, self-improvement, the inner workings of the CIA, or even Workers Comp insurance (all topics on which I've co-authored books). All of this informa-tion is valuable as source material for the fiction that I write. As someone once said of James Joyce, every-thing was "grist for his mill." I feel the same way. Everything is useable. If I help someone write a cook-book, what I learn from the experience will come in handy at some point in my fiction.

Co-authoring also reinforces my narrative skills. With almost everything I write, I still need to impose a structure, a pace, a narrative line, and a unique voice. In fact, ghostwriting a book is a lot like creating a char-acter's voice (the nominal "author") that requires consistency, depth, authenticity—all those qualities you try to imbue a fictional character with.

A colleague recently asked me if it wasn't demeaning to "subordinate" myself to someone else's content, becoming in his words, "not much more than a transcriber." As I hope my comments here make clear, I don't feel that way at all. Rather, I feel as though I'm providing a valuable service, almost like a translator or facilitator. In the bargain, I'm well compensated and I'm essentially doing research all the time, building a store of knowledge that will enrich my body of work.

Paul L. Hall
President & CEO
PrecisionProse, a Paul L. Hall & Associates Company

Law #4

The query letter should always initially be used to gain the interest of those in the publishing industry.

L ET'S SAY THAT IT'S CHRISTMAS DAY OR HANUKKAH. YOU'VE taken weeks to prepare a spread that should grace the cover of *Holiday Meals Magazine*. Everyone is there — dozens of close friends and family who have come in from all across the globe.

Smiling from ear to ear, you are just about to proudly present the food to your cherished, famished herd, when the doorbell rings. Thinking that it may be a late-arriving guest, you rush over, open the door, and find me, whom you have never seen before, standing there, toothy grin, hair flowing way beyond my shoulders, with arched collar, black leather jacket, and all.

Expecting Uncle Hank or Bud, Aunt Vi or someone else you love and adore to be making a last-minute, surprise appearance, you are caught completely off guard by me, the stranger at the door. As a result, you don't really know what to say.

"Ah, yes," you mumble under your breath, "may I help you?"

"Yes," I reply, as cocky and confident as can be. "The reason that I am here," I say, reaching for your arm, "is because I would like you to leave with me immediately to do fifty hours of free, physical labor."

You don't know what to say, but you're sure as heck that you don't want to go. So, you pull back, utter a few polite apologies, and softly close the door in my face.

You then turn, relief gracing your face, and head back to reignite the festivities simply with the glow of your personality, when the doorbell rings again. You slowly and reluctantly turn back and peek out of the peephole in the door to see me standing there again, only this time, there are now a dozen long-haired, smiling, at least slightly warped, literary types, all looking straight toward you, mouthing the same exact request I had beseeched you with only moments before.

Somehow, you dodge the bullet again, only to be called to the threshold of your home every five minutes by an even larger gathering of persons, looking like me and all mouthing the same request. Eventually, you lose it. Maybe you start screaming obscenities. Maybe you call the cops. Either way, you find yourself responding completely out of character.

What does a scenario such as this have to do with your publishing aspirations as a would-be author?

Everything.

Yes! Tom, I just received a 'please send us your book and submission package for review' on 'The Golden Ones'!
Carole, student, Virginia

You see, were you to follow the normal procedure subscribed to by most new writers, you'd wind up experiencing the same fate as my friends and me camped out on your lawn. The last thing that an editor or literary agent wants to see appear on his or her desk is an un-requested, full-length manuscript from an unrecognized, new author. The reality is that there is barely time for editors and agents to read the books that they are contractually obligated to review.

The Simple Truth

As successful as the majority of aspiring authors happen to be in the other aspects of their lives, few if any proceed beyond their mistake of sending their hard-earned manuscript off to a publishing house, which is almost certain to reject it. Yet unbeknownst to them, the roots of their rejections spring not from the lack of quality of their work, but instead from violating a simple but essential, unwritten etiquette of the literary world.

Let's frame this situation in a real-life context so as to better help you understand. If you wanted to land a job with a respected company or corporation, you couldn't expect much, if any, success if you just walked into their headquarters and demanded a high-ranking, executive position or any other job. In most cases, if you were to do that you would be lucky just to be thrown out onto the street. Wouldn't it make sense that if you were to emulate the same action in the literary arena by firing off your manuscript to a publishing house without first going through the proper channels that you would meet with the same results? Of course.

So to best dodge such an unnecessary rejection, wouldn't it make sense that maybe you should follow a system comparable to the one utilized in the job place-ment field? Of course.

In most cases, when you apply for a job you are expected to submit a personal letter and résumé. The literary arena has its own version of that as well. However, in the literary marketplace, rarely is its version sent directly to potential publishers. Because of the usually high traffic volume, it is instead sent to an essential middleman who fills the same role as a headhunter or job placement counselor, called a literary agent.

The query letter package is analogous to the use of a résumé in the job market. Just as a résumé secures a job interview, the Query Letter Package secures a literary interview with an editor or agent for your work. This point is important enough to be made again: A Query Letter Package doesn't sell one's work; it simply gives a writer the opportunity he or she needs to sell his or her work. That's all.

Using it greatly increases your chance of a sale. Ignoring it vastly increases your chance of failure. In fact, inappropriately introducing yourself and your idea to a potential source by sending your manuscript directly will almost certainly lead to rejection. So, if you've been impatiently contemplating saying, "To hell with the query letter," and just submitting the manuscript you've written, don't do it. No matter how good your material is, you'll only be setting yourself up for failure.

I'm still getting positive replies from agents on my query letter package. I got yet another one during the week of the 13th.
Dorothy, student, Scottsdale, Arizona

The Query Letter Package Allows You to Gauge the Depth of Any Potential Interest in a Project.

If you send out a query and find there is enough interest in your project to devote your time, energy, and potentially money to it, great! If there isn't much or any interest, the query letter can save you from wasting any further resources.

Positive responses to your Query Letter Package build confidence in your project and your approach to your writing.

This added confidence will not only show itself in your writing style, but the savvy with which you approach the publishing of your material.

The Query Letter Package Prevents Creative Constipation.

That's right, creative constipation. If you're anything like me, and I have to believe that you are, ideas are probably flowing through your mind all the time. If you don't find some way to release them, they'll get backed up. As a result, you'll lose your ability to identify what your creative mind is trying to share with you. You'll get frustrated and angry, negatively reinforcing any output from your creative mind and severely preventing its future attempts to communicate with you.

By properly utilizing a query letter, which is relatively easy to write once you get the hang of it, you will be putting those ideas to use, freeing yourself of the dreaded creative constipation.

Sending a Query Letter Package Is FUN

There is no pressure involved. If whomever you contact likes your idea...great! Then, and only then, shall you give serious consideration to actually producing your product. If they don't like your idea, you can either review your query letter and send it elsewhere or dump the idea. Besides a small amount of your time, a little work on the Internet, and/or a few stamps, a bit of stationery, and a few envelopes, you don't have much to lose.

The Query Letter

The Two Types of Query Letters

You will send a query letter for Fiction or Non-Fiction. There is no special design that needs to be adhered to for different genres. What you are writing is either fiction or non-fiction. Period. Though both the fiction and non-fiction query letters are made up of five separate parts, each one has its own unique design. Samples follow in Appendix B at the end of the book.

The Most Important Elements to Keep in Mind About the Query Letter:

- The query should always be neatly typed.
- Limit the query to one page in length.
- Limit the size of your paragraphs, giving it the appearance of a quick, easy read.
- Include your name, address, and telephone number.

The Five Elements of a Fiction Query Letter

1. The Title

Most new writers erroneously spend far too much time choosing a title for their project. They innocently believe that whatever title they commit to for their query will eventually become the title of their book, which is not true. In fact, it is not unusual for a title to change several times before a final choice is made. Professionals in the literary business are well aware of this, so they won't hold you to any of your initial impulses.

For the purpose of a query letter, it is essential that the title merely attract a reader's interest. That's all. Just come up with something that will grab your potential reader's attention.

2. The Grabber

The Grabber comprises the first paragraph of a fictional query letter. It should be no more than three short sentences in length. Its purpose is to further entice the reader to review the remainder of your query. No matter how good your query may be later, if you lose an editor or agent here, they won't read the rest. Your work will thus be returned to you without ever having gotten a fair chance to be seen.

Here are three suggestions to better aid you in this area.

First: stay away from beginning a query letter with a question. Your readers simply won't know enough about your characters or your story in general to care about the answer to your question.

Second: the key to effective fiction is to get your readers to feel. Thus, the best way to grab their attention is to appeal to as many of their five senses as possible. Create an interesting image for your readers to get lost in, and you will have them hooked.

Third: to give your readers a better idea of the potential of your work, compare the eventual success of your proposed project with a literary success.

3. The Characters

Before you can share anything with your agent, editor, or publisher about your proposed work, it is essential that you first identify your top two or three characters. Your goal with each character description is to: a) create the proper imagery to bring the character to life in your reader's mind, and b) to begin to gently introduce the storyline or plot of your prospective work.

4. The Plot or Storyline

The next portion of your query should be used to share your plot or storyline with the reader.

5. The Ending

Use the last paragraph to leave your prospective audience with something to remember you and/or your project by.

The Five Elements of a Non-Fiction Query Letter

1. The Title

The purpose and reason behind the title in a non-fiction query letter is exactly the same as its fictional counterpart. It is meant to attract attention. It need not necessarily be considered your final title. In fact, what you choose as your title at this stage will probably change several times before your work appears in print. So, don't place undue pressure upon yourself by sweating over a title. Come up with something appropriate that attracts a reader's attention and go with that.

2. The Grabber

Catch your reader's attention with a comparison-evoking statement as was alluded to in the description of the fictional query letter. An example of this technique can be found in the sample non-fiction query letter in Appendix B.

3. Markets

Where good imagery catches a reader's attention in a fictional query letter, the identification of a significant population that would be interested in reading your work, how large that audience is, and what void in the literary world you will be filling with your project, accomplishes this in the non-fiction query letter. Besides your primary audience, list anyone else you think would be interested in reading about your topic.

4. The Makeup and Design of Your Project

This is where you give agents, editors, and publishers a quick but enlightening rundown of some of the chapter headings, sectional breakdowns, and topics to be covered in your work.

5. The Ending

As with the fictional query letter, leave your readers with something favorable by which to remember you and/or your project.

Salutations and Such

Personalize your approach with either type of query by using the name of the literary agent and agency, or editor and publisher. Sign off at the bottom in your usual manner and by promising to provide anyone interested in seeing more material with whatever they request.

Credentials

Don't jam up your query letter with a long list of credits, degrees, and credentials, if you have any. Simply list any pertinent degrees in your letterhead and quickly mention any credits or credentials in no more than a sentence or two at the conclusion of your letter.

The last quarter of a century of my life has been pretty constantly and faithfully devoted to the study of the human race—that is to say, the study of myself, for in the individual person I am the entire human race compacted together. I have found that there is no ingredient of the race which I do not possess in either a small way or a large way.

Mark Twain

Success Story by Rhonda Jones

From: Rhonda Jones, Knoxville, Tennessee
To: Tom Bird
Author: *Teaching Common Sense*, (Bright Hope Productions)

"No doubt about it, when I heard Tom say, 'I may die a fool, but I won't die a coward,' I made the choice on the spot at forty-one years of age to finally follow my dream. Within a month after taking his course, I had entered into Tom's Intensive Writer's Program and begun writing my first book. I remember well how scared and apprehensive I was in the beginning. . . afraid Tom would think I couldn't write. . .afraid I didn't have a book in me. . .afraid that I wouldn't have the time to maintain the discipline Tom expected. . .afraid that even if I could be a writer, I couldn't make a living. . .I was even afraid that Tom wouldn't live up to his end of the bargain. But like any fresh convert, I acted purely on faith. Whenever those fears tried to creep back in, I simply reminded myself that I didn't choose this destiny. It chose me. God has chosen to speak through me. Who am I to argue with that? All my worries were for naught. Exactly one year later my first book is published! I simply cannot believe how much I've learned in that relatively short amount of time. I feel so comfortable now in this writer's skin I was born to wear and in this industry I've learned to navigate. There will always be mountains to climb and hurdles to jump, but I now have the knowledge and confidence to never let up. That's a feeling I never thought I would know. Tom Bird did that for me. Tom believed in me, even before he knew a thing about me. It is his belief, his passion, his no-nonsense style, his discipline, his encouragement, his relentlessness, and his enlightened approach that have transformed me into the person I was always meant to be. Tom and his approach are truly divinely inspired. Thanks to Tom Bird, I am Rhonda Jones, author.

Law #5

**For books and screenplays,
always approach literary
agents with your query letters.**

THE GOOD NEWS IS THAT THERE ARE THOUSANDS OF
independent firms in this country who claim to
perform the services of literary agents.

The bad news is that even though there are a few
governing bodies that attempt to do so, there is no univer-
sally accepted ethical body, like the American Medical
Association for the medical field, that determines who is
and who is not qualified to be a literary agent. What this
means, in my estimation, is that over three-quarters of
those individuals who call themselves literary agents fall
way short of the title, or in the worst cases, are downright
frauds.

How Can You Tell?

First, a literary agent is a commission-based salesperson.

Second, he or she has the expertise to help you edit and
refine your writing for submission to publishing houses.

Third, literary agents fill the role of literary legal counsel. He or she negotiates and enforces your literary contracts.

How do you know whether an agent is a potential fraud? Quite simply, if they charge for any of the above services, be very, very leery.

Beware of false prophets, which come to you in sheep's clothing, but inwardly they are ravening wolves...

Matthew 7:15

Let's take that point a little further.

Let us say that a prospective agent's name is Bob. Bob has expressed an interest in reviewing your manuscript for potential representation to a publisher.

Bob reminds you, however, "Don't forget to send along the $1,200 reading fee with your manuscript."

Many so-called literary agents charge reading fees, not to subsidize an outside service to review your material but instead to supplement their incomes because they are not making enough money, if any, selling works to publishers. What then does that tell you about Bob's ability as a literary salesperson? Right. He has little, if any, and he certainly is not the type of person you want handling your literary gem.

The same goes with editing fees.

The biggest come-on in the latter part of the last century in the literary industry was staged when a number of so-called editing services began contacting literary agents with an offer many of the latter couldn't refuse. Since the once-unsuspecting audience of aspiring authors had begun to catch on to the reading fee game, these editing services decided to offer teetering agencies an opportunity to significantly subsidize their meager incomes. All these agencies had to do was recommend the services of the editing service. If a referral from one of the agencies signed on with the editorial firm, the agency was given anywhere from a 30%-40% kickback from the fees charged by the editing service.

Pretty sweet deal, huh? For the unethical agency and editing service maybe, but not for the innocent writer who in most cases was led to believe, by the agency, that all that was needed to achieve publication was one good, thorough edit. Unfortunately though, even if that were the case, it would have been impossible with any of the aforementioned firms, who in most cases used high school seniors and college underclassmen to revise and edit the manuscripts they received.

Where to Find That Right Agent

There are plenty of listings of literary agents available.

- The *Literary Marketplace* (LMP): The Directory of the American Book Publishing Industry, as it is referred to by its publisher, can be found in almost any library. Though it offers the names, addresses, and telephone numbers, as well as a small description of approximately 400 literary agents, the majority of the information on each literary agent is meant for use by proven professionals within the field. Thus, the descriptions are often of little use to the new writer.

- Publishersmarketplace.com: Offers in-depth descriptions on dozens of the top agencies as well as information about some of the best book editors, publicists, etc. The cost is $20 a month to subscribe, which includes a daily newsletter emailed out to you. An invaluable and highly recommended source.

- Mediabistro.com: Offers many in depth descriptions of literary agents, editors, etc. The cost to subscribe is approximately $50 a year. A highly recommended source, worthy of looking into.

- Independent Listings: Libraries often carry general listings of literary agents that have been published over the years. But oftentimes the addresses and telephone numbers listed in such publications are outdated, so check carefully. There are also a variety of Internet sources of this type available.

- Tom Bird's Selective Guide to Literary Agents Database: Specifically designed for use by the new author, it boasts a listing of over 800 top literary agents who don't charge fees and who are open to accepting new clients. For your convenience and in an effort to save you time and money, the Literary Guide is offered as a database only. More information on it can be found on my website or by calling my office at 928-203-0265.

How to Choose That Right Agent

The acquisition of the proper literary representative is paramount to your success in this field. Allow me to STRESS again, that it is of the utmost importance to find the right literary agent for YOU.

Each literary agent is different. Each one has different qualities, likes, dislikes, and approaches. As with any partnership, the right literary agent will make you. The wrong one can break you. Thus it is important that you don't just take the first literary agent that happens along and offers you representation. No. It is important that your decision for the choice of a literary agent be based upon a significant amount of comparative research.

To evaluate a literary agent for possible contact, you should consider each of the following:

- Area of Expertise: Do they handle the type of material you want to write?

- Are They Taking on New Clients? If they are not willing to take on anyone new, there's no reason to contact them.

- Versatility: How many different types of books a literary agent represents is very important. For example, if you choose an agent who only works with romance novels, and then after he or she sells your first Harlequin you get an impulse to write a cookbook, you will have to go outside your present agent for representation.

- Contacts: Does the agents you are considering have developed contacts at the major publishing houses?

- Commission Rate: What commission rate do they charge? Ten percent or fifteen [or "10% or 15%"]?

- Clout: Do they represent important writers so publishers pay attention to them? What new clients do they represent?

- Sales Ratio: This information is hard to come by,

but if you can acquire it, it will prove the most beneficial of all criteria considered. Defined, a sales ratio for a literary agent is simply the number of books sold per year per client. If a literary agent has 30 clients and sold 15 books last year, he or she averages one-half of a book sale per year per client represented, which is an outstanding ratio.

- Size: Small literary agents, with fifty clients or fewer, are oftentimes new in the business, hungrier, and willing to offer you more of their time than larger agents, who represent 150 clients or more. But the presence of larger, older, and, thus, more established agents usually have an inside track.

- Location: To be able to have a profitable working relationship with a literary agent, it is important that you are able to get along with them. A specific location oftentimes determines a person's attitude and approach to life. At times, location also determines specialty. Make sure that you strongly consider this when shopping for an agent.

Finding a Literary Agent for Your Book

Step One

Go to one (or more than one) of the listings of literary agents mentioned in this chapter. Then, based upon the criteria that was shared with you in that same section, choose at least 200 agencies (remember it is essential to be thorough to be successful in this arena) that you feel, for one reason or another, would be valid representatives for you. Then, based upon what you learned from reading their descriptions, and even more so on how you intuitively feel about each one, arrange your listing from the literary agent you think would be best for you to the one you feel would be the least best for you.

In heaven an angel is nobody in particular.

George Bernard Shaw

Step Two

Forward your Query Letter Package to your entire listing at the same time. Then sit back and wait for their replies.

It's decision-making time, but, as you will see, a very easy one to make. What you need to do before moving on is to decide which one of two potential methods you will employ to submit your query letter package.

The first alternative is to send your material via the old US Post Office, commonly referred to by those in the cyber world as snail mail. In this regard, snail mail translates to individually addressing each of your 200 or more letters, individually labeling them, stuffing them, and purchasing both mailing postage and return postage for each source chosen. So, not only is it monetarily expensive, but it could take dozens of hours to complete as well.

Now, up until just a few months after 9/11, that was about your only alternative. But then, during those months when the publishing/literary industry almost completely shut down, something changed in the psyches of literary agents everywhere. That is when, in greater numbers than ever before, agents became open to accepting e-mailed query letter packages.

Even though I was thrilled when this trend finally appeared, I was still a bit skeptical. So, I e-mailed several query letters to ensure that this trend was indeed real and here to stay. To my amazement, not only was the percentage of positive replies to the query letters nearly eight times higher than what I would have normally expected to receive via snail mailed versions, but on an average over 60% of those contacted replied within forty-eight hours.

So, your choice is really clear-cut. Choosing your literary agents from a database and e-mailing them out takes about twenty minutes as opposed to an average of eighteen to twenty hours via the snail mail route. Outside the purchase of the database listing (and you would have to acquire some sort of listing for the snail mail route as well), it costs absolutely nothing to mail out your 200+ queries. Going the snail mail route, with return postage included, will cost you $148 to send out 200 queries. Response time? You'll begin receiving responses within hours via the e-mail alternative and will have the vast majority of your replies back in your hands in days. The snail mail approach? It will take you an average of six to eight weeks before you can count on having received the majority of your replies.

Now, I realize that there are some of you who still do not feel comfortable with using the computer, let alone the Internet. But the e-mail alternative is so much faster, more efficient, cheaper, and more successful that I cannot help but highly recommend it. If you don't yet feel comfortable with your computer or the Internet, why not have a friend or a family member who is a bit more cyber savvy submit your package for you?

If you are submitting your query letter through the Internet, you can expect an almost instant reply from a good portion of your list, and you will receive replies from approximately 50% of those you contacted within ten days.

Step Three

Wait. After you've received your first offer to review, the next step is to sit back and collect acceptances, or work on another Query Letter Package in a non-competing field. There's nothing else that can be done until you have heard, whether they replied affirmatively or not, from at least 50% of your sources. If after ten days there are still agents who you have yet to hear from, resubmit your query letter to those agencies.

What Type of Responses You Can Expect From Literary Agents

Through the proper utilization of this system, you can expect not to receive any rejections from literary agents. That doesn't mean that every literary agent will want to see more of your book/screenplay, it just means that you won't receive any of the harsh rejections of one's character or abilities you may have heard your friends receiving, or which you may have even been subjected to yourself. The reason for that is simple: by employing the methods shared in this book, not only will you be projecting your-self professionally, but you will also be doing so within the lines of the unwritten etiquette of the industry. So if you are looking for some harsh slams against either you or your work, you won't be receiving them.

What you can expect to receive are positive replies to your query letters. What do positive replies translate to?

A positive reply to your query letter from a literary agent constitutes a request for you to submit either a submission package, some sample material from your manuscript, or your entire book/screenplay.

How many can you expect?

Approximately 50% of the agents you query will respond within ten days. So if you queried 200 literary agents, you can expect to hear from about 100 of those within a week and a half.

Of those replying, how many can you expect to respond positively?

Since the income of these representatives is commissioned-based, they have to be very selective in regard to whom they take on as clients. With that said, approximately a 4% rate of positive replies would be considered excellent, which means if you heard back from 100 agents, you could expect four to reply positively to your query.

To substantially increase this number, I strongly suggest sending your query to as many agents as possible. For example, my selective guide to literary agents would allow you to submit to upwards of four hundred agents or more if you were writing adult fiction or nonfiction.

Even with that taken into consideration though, remember that you only need to land one agent. More importantly, it is essential that he or she is the "right" agent.

Examples of typical responses from literary agents follow in Appendix C.

Law #6

**You need to hook a literary agent with the
proper submission package to
land the representation you need.**

H ERE ARE SOME IMPORTANT THINGS TO KEEP IN MIND ABOUT
this stage:

1. It may take from a few days to several months for
   an agent to review your material and get back to
   you.

2. Because of the number of submission packages
   received by an agent, it is recommended that you
   follow up with a courtesy phone call to ensure
   that your material was received.

Submitting Your Book Idea

*Reviewing, Evaluating, and, Most of All,
Standardizing Your Agent Responses*

If you have sent out your Query Letter Packages on
your book and you have begun receiving responses, you

have probably already come to an understanding of just how schizophrenic an industry this happens to be.

First, your sources replied in a wide variety of ways, ranging from an email, neatly typed letter, or polite telephone call (telephone calls are very rare and should be taken as a sign directly from God) to sloppily handwritten notes. **Second**, they probably are far from what you expected them to be.

Still, it is very important to pay very close attention to your immediate reaction to each response, as this will serve as a true and accurate key to help you better understand exactly what type of person and/or agency your literary soul is leading you to, or away from.

So, budget some time in a very relaxed space to look over your acceptances. While doing this, on a separate piece of paper, spontaneously list each agency offering an acceptance . Then rate your agents, giving each a score from a low of "1" to a high of "10," based on two factors: their enthusiasm for your work, and how strongly you feel about each one. Then add those two figures together. The sum you come up with will allow you to rank them from whom you like best to whom you like least.

The Submission Package

Before we go any further, let me first clarify that a submission package, no matter what shape, size, or design it takes, is put together after receiving positive replies to your Query Letter Package from a literary agent. If he or she is interested in you and in your work after reviewing your submission package, there is a good chance that you will be offered a contract.

Once that happens, your agent will normally help you refine your submission package to attract publishers. After that is completed, it is sent off for sale.

The proposal is utilized for non-fiction projects about which you cannot assume your readers will have more than a passing understanding. Thus, a more elaborate introduction of the subject matter is needed. This introduction is spread throughout the multitude of variables that make up the Proposal Package.

The thorough introduction of the necessary topic, via a Proposal Package, is addressed across several categories, listed below. Most of these components will be replicated in the other two submission packages, the Synopsis Package, and the Children's Book Package. So, except where a separate clarification and/or introduction is necessary and is included, the description of the majority of the following will transfer, quite nicely, for use in the other areas as well.

For an even more elaborate study of what a Proposal Package is and what it should look like, I strongly suggest reading a copy of Michael Larsen's *How to Write a Book Proposal*.

1. A Title Page

2. A Table of Contents

3. A One-Page Bio on the Author or a Curriculum Vitae

4. An Overview or Synopsis, giving a general idea of what is being proposed and why

5. The Market

6. A Chapter-by-Chapter Sketch of the book

7. Competition

8. A Collection of Sample Work from the book

To enable you to best understand the elements of these packages, following are more elaborate descriptions of the above elements.

Title Page

This should include the working title of your book, a designation on whether it is fiction or nonfiction, your name, address, phone number and email address.

Table of Contents

This is the Table of Contents for your Submission Package, not for your book.

Author Bio

The purpose of the one-page bio is to introduce the author, or authors, of a proposed work to a literary agent. To successfully compose a bio, a few points must always be highlighted:

- Identify what attributes make you the best writer for this piece.

- List any writing credentials or experiences that convey some authority in the field you are writing about; or, if neither of those are possible, at least show or illustrate a significant amount of commitment that you have already made to the art of writing, even if that means just having kept a journal for the last twenty years.

- Specify the direction of your future interests.

Sample Title Page

A Proposal for

The Heart's Way

Being Good Enough
The Key to Unlocking Inner Peace

OR

The Heart's Way

Do you or someone you know need to
get back to who you really are or
discover yourself for the first time?

By Dr. Sharon Lamm-Hartman

Dr. Sharon Lamm-Hartman
PO Box 1234
Yourtown, USA
123-456-7890
author@msn.com
www.insideoutlearninginc.com

It is usually best to organize the above into three separate paragraphs. The use of the third person is also highly recommended over first person. It is much easier to cover large amounts of ground quicker in that manner. It is also essential that the bio you write display your style and character. Don't try to copy anybody here. Cheap imitations never sell in the literary world. Be yourself, and let them see who you are.

The Overview or Synopsis

The book overview used for non-fiction is composed of the same five components that make up a query. In essence, it is a long, long query letter designed to entertainingly answer all questions that a literary agent could potentially ask. To be an effective writer, it is essential that several topics be approached and expounded upon, most of which should have been covered already in the aforementioned exercise and can be conveniently converted for use in your book overview. They are:

1. What is your idea for a book?
2. Who is your audience?
3. Why will your book be a valuable asset to your audience?
4. What do you hope to accomplish with the writing of your book?
5. What ideas do you have for the potential sale and promotion of the book?
6. How many words do you expect the book to be?
7. What are you willing to do to participate in the promotion of the book?

8. How long will it take you to fully complete the writing of the book?

Examples of an overview for your review are included in the sample Proposal Packages later in this chapter.

∽

Like the book proposal, the synopsis, which is employed for fiction, is a long query letter. But it is important that your synopsis successfully achieve two very important goals.

First and foremost, the synopsis must carry with it the tone and creative tension of your book. To do this, simply expand the thoroughly shortened storyline or plot, the fourth component, that you shared in your query letter. Again, remember, it's important to make your tale come to life by routinely evoking all of the reader's five senses.

Second, it is necessary that the topics listed above for the Overview also be effectively, but not necessarily directly, addressed in the Synopsis.

Market

In your opinion, who is going to purchase your book? Who makes up your primary audience? Your secondary audience? List these sources.

Competition

This is where you compare the potential of your book with other books that have been published on the same subject. To do this, start out by making a broad general statement in regard to how your book compares, such as: "The following twelve books have been published in the lat ten years on the same subject I will be addressing in my book, proving that there is a market for the work I am proposing. Where my book varies greatly from the following works is that: 1) my work is up-to-date in regard to all the information being furnished; 2) my work offers greater reader interaction through quizzes, exercises and assignments, a must in today's proactive world; and 3) it is far more in depth than any of the works which follow."

Follow up your opening statement to this section with a quick one or two sentence description of each work along with a listing of not only the title and author's name of each book, but its copyright date, publisher, whether it was initially printed in hardback or paperback and price.

The Chapter-by-Chapter Sketch

The chapter-by-chapter sketch gives a literary agent a more detailed idea of how your book will be composed. The main focus of the chapter-by-chapter sketch is to share enough to give your authoritative reader a deeper understanding of the content of each chapter without telling so much that it winds up boring him or her.

Sample Work

No matter what you've offered literary agents up to this point in your submission package, how well you pull off this section spells make-or-break time.

There are two things that a literary agent will look for in any sample chapters you include. **First** of all, they will want to see how quickly you grab your reader's attention. **Second**, they want to see how effectively you communicate and carry your story forward.

The Nonfiction Submission Package or Proposal Package

The Proposal Package is normally broken up into the following components:

1. Title Page
2. Table of Contents for the Submission Package
3. Overview
4. Market
4. Competition
5. Chapter-by-Chapter Sketch
6. Author's Bio
7. Sample Material

Sample Submission Packages are available in the back of the book in Appendix D.

The Submission Package for Adult Fiction

Elements of a Submission Package for Adult Fiction

The following must be included in a submission package for a book of adult fiction:

1. A Title Page
2. A Table of Contents
3. A Synopsis
4. A Chapter-by-Chapter Sketch
5. An Author's Bio or Curriculum Vitae
6. Sample Material

A sample synopsis follows on the next page.

Sample Synopsis

Places the Dead Call Home
By Paul L. Hall

Synopsis

On a summer night in 1958, bullets tear through the body of a young man on a lonely Oklahoma highway. Nineteen years later, a soldier lies in the pool of his own blood on an army base in Virginia. Death has made room at home for both of them. Death can always find room for more.

Josh Kincaid is a common link to both events. In 2002, when Kincaid's cousin proposes an urgent trip to the Anasazi ruins of Mesa Verde to resolve the riddle of one of these deaths, Kincaid reluctantly agrees. Soon, he and a van full of misfits are on the way to the cliff dwellings of the "ancestral enemies," where flesh-and-blood enemies await them among the ruins.

This sets the stage for Places the Dead Call Home.

Josh Kincaid is happy with life in Phoenix where he manages a bar and sells a few drugs on the side His serenity is soon shattered, however, by a call from his cousin, Frankie McKnight, who claims to know why Josh's father died many years earlier far from his Detroit home in the parking lot of a gas station in Oklahoma City.

General Herman Endicott is looking for Josh, too. The highlight of his military life was winning the Silver Star for bravery in Vietnam, followed a few years later by his promotion to General. But between those events, the death of a

---

friend and the betrayal of an old comrade have brought disgrace to a bereaved widow and her unborn child. This secret could destroy the General, and Josh Kincaid may know that secret.

General Endicott hires Tommy Three Hands, an Indian living in the Phoenix area, to kill Josh and Frankie, along with a reporter named Jeffrey Bonus and his traveling companion, Jeanette Koskos, who have also shown up with questions about the death of Bonus's father. Tommy is an ex-con who distrusts and hates whites, enjoys a reputation for violence and betrayal, and has a cruel streak when it comes to women. He also has a grudge against Josh and his cousin Frankie.

All of these characters converge on Mesa Verde, where the secret of the mysterious—and perhaps violent—disappearance of the Anasazi still seems to inhabit the ruins. As Josh and Frankie seek the answer to Jimmy Kincaid's destiny in the park's mythic heritage and Bonus hopes to learn the true fate of his father, Tommy and the General are making plans of their own to ensure that the dead stay where they belong—the places they call home.

The Submission Package for Children's Books

Elements of a Submission Package for a Children's Book

1. A Title Page
2. A Table of Contents for the Submission Package
3. An Author's Bio
4. A One-Page Description of Potential Markets
5. Your Completed Manuscript
6. A Sample Illustration, if you choose to include one

As you can see, no synopsis, book proposal, or chapter-by-chapter sketch is included. The inclusion of any of the above would be foolish. The inclusion of the entire manuscript should speak for itself.

Including a Sample Illustration

Only include a sample illustration if you are capable of either illustrating your book yourself or if you already have an artist whom you plan to use. Please also be aware that only an 8 1/2" x 11" black-and-white sample illustration needs to be included. In addition, you should also know that less than half of potential children's book publishers accept outside illustrators. Most prefer to use their own. Thus the literary agents you are submitting to may be cool on the idea as well. But don't let this deter you if you are either determined to illustrate your own book, or if you have an artist outside of the publishing industry you are determined to work with.

Preparing to Create
the Submission Package

An Energy and Timesaving Exercise

The first rule in composing a submission package is that you have to make your educated, professional readers FEEL that what you have to offer is worthy of their time, and at the same time aid them in understanding the potential of your project. To do this can seem an insurmountable task. In fact, no other activity has caused my students more strife. However, I have a solution for dealing with that dilemma.

I find that all those who come to me, after going through the exercises at the beginning of this book, receive a vision or an image in their mind, one of great completeness, which offers all that they need to know to understand their thrust of, and reason behind, their desires to write. Communicating this under the pressure of review and judgment as a submission package by literary agents is another thing altogether.

In the vast majority of cases, the pressure upon even the finest writers was far too great. They cracked, some unable to write at all. Many never made it beyond this point. Those who did oftentimes had to work through dozens of drafts to regain their well-formed literary voices, which had been avalanched by their overreactions to the situation.

I knew that there had to be an easier way around this dilemma, something that would enable them to retain their literary voices and complete the necessary work smoothly and efficiently. It was during one of my lectures on the topic that the inspiration came to me.

Why not have them form the basis for writing their synopsis or proposal, the components they struggled with the most, by composing a letter to a close friend, with whom they obviously would feel very comfortable?

Yes, that was it! It has been a long-recognized fact that we have always done our finest writing when communicating with someone that we know and trust. If we simply approached a close and dear comrade with a letter describing what we wanted to do and how we were going to do it, not only would our most natural voice reveal itself, but the style would only have to be altered slightly to become the synopsis or proposal that we wanted it to be.

The technique worked so well that I have been using it ever since, saving aspiring writers dozens of useless drafts and, in the most extreme cases, keeping the vast majority of those I work with from giving up in the face of the rigors of this step.

To best activate this technique, get in a deep relaxed state. Upon opening your eyes, begin your letter with the words, "Dear ___, I have a great idea for a book."

Then take off. Let your passions for your idea be your guide. Empty yourself onto the paper. Leave no stone unturned. Act as if it has been a substantial time since you have last spoken to your friend and that he or she knows nothing about your idea.

Describe how the book idea came to you. If it's fiction, describe who the characters are; if it's non-fiction, who you think will buy it and how it would best be promoted. Mention why you feel that you are the best writer to author this story. Empty your soul onto paper. Let it all hang out.

In the following sample, just such a letter has been included. Remember it is very rough and doesn't in any way showcase the author's exceptionally refined ability. But, hopefully, from reading it, you will grasp the understanding behind this unique, idea-formulating technique.

I've been writing for over eight years without having completed what I wanted to successfully write. Three-and-a-half months after the Intensive Writer's Retreat, my book is done and a second is halfway finished. The ME that I met head-on in the retreat was set free to write.

Isabella Quigley, student, Jacksonville, Florida

Sample Brainstorming Letter

Dear Tom,

I have a great idea for a book about when people learn to think reflectively. From my years in the classroom, I learned that when students think superficially and do not get involved with the task, they score poorly. A good memory will get students high scores on multiple-choice tests without the benefit of really learning or understanding much. Students learn to play the game of school, sometimes spending more time avoiding involvement than it would take to learn the lesson. These students, and I think they are the majority, graduate from high school with little reading and writing practice, getting by with doing as little as possible. Although they may or may not go to college, they are not lifelong learners. I call these passive learners "aliterates" because although they are able to decode and encode, it is in the area of comprehension that their thinking skills are lacking.

Actually, I want you to know that this is not only my opinion; the National Assessment of Educational Progress has found plenty of evidence. In fact, the great school reform movement in the late 80s was a direct result of these test scores, which revealed that students could read and write, but they were not very good at thinking. If you remember, there were several books concerned with education on the bestseller list. You probably remember Cultural Literacy, Frames of Mind, Among Schoolchildren, High School, The Closing of the American Mind. Responses to these publications indicate that there is presently a national concern for teaching and learning in American schools.

Unfortunately, I have to add that my work at the college level with student teachers and their cooperating teachers has given me reason to believe that many teachers are not "thinkers" either. Kids need role models. "Do as I say, not as I do," doesn't work well. Recently I read a book by Howard Gardner entitled, The Unschooled Mind (1991), which really made an impression on me. Anyway, Gardner writes, "Children read not because they are told — let alone ordered to read, but because they see adults around them reading, enjoying their reading, and using that reading productively for their own purposes, ranging from assembling a piece of apparatus to laughing at a tall tale." I am convinced that this is true, not only when it comes to reading, but also, to thinking.

There is one more thing I want to mention that brought me to the point of thinking that I could write a book about thinking. You see, I have been thinking about thinking for some time now. The term educators use when they discuss "thinking about thinking" is metacognition, which means that a person can be aware of his own thinking processes. In other words, I'm sure you have talked to yourself or questioned your own motives for doing something. I tell my student teachers that it is one thing to recall the lesson or to describe what the kids did, but they have an added benefit if they think about the students' perspective, or what they could have done differently, or if time could have been spent more wisely. I heard a teacher say once, "Boy, the whole class did poorly on that test. Those kids must not have studied;" the idea that it may have been a "poor" test never entered the teacher's mind.

Secondly, along the same line, I have done a great deal of research on writing. I wrote my dissertation on writing, I go to conventions on writing, I attend seminars on writing, and occasionally, I do writing workshops for English teachers. My doctoral degree is in language communications, and I am well aware of the theoretical and practical approaches to teaching and learning reading and writing. Furthermore, everything that I have been reading lately connects writing to thinking.

The last thing I need to bring up is what teachers refer to as Bloom's Taxonomy of Educational Objectives, which describes six levels of cognition. The levels are 1) knowledge—recall information, 2) comprehension—summarize or paraphrase, 3) application—relate to a prior experience, 4) analysis—classify, categorize, compare parts, 5) synthesis—put together in a new way, and 6) evaluation—make informed judgments and support opinion. Originally, the taxonomy was thought of as a hierarchy, meaning that you had to teach at level one before going to level two, but today it is used as a simple way to look at how thinking skills are related to teaching and learning. However, there is plenty of research to indicate that what we teach in schools is mainly lower-level thinking, tasks that require recall and paraphrase at the knowledge and comprehension levels. Generally, we think of application, analysis, synthesis, and evaluation as higher-order thinking skills. Perhaps this is another reason that students score poorly on higher-level thinking skills.

The good news is, we do know how to teach and learn these skills. It seems to me that most of us reach a point in time when we realize that it is important to think clearly, or at least we see a need for being a better thinker. How many times have you said, "I just didn't think." The drunk driver has said it. The inexperienced hunter has said it. Young mothers have said it. Probably, the Vice-President has said it. Habits of thinking can be improved quite easily. For example, if your child complains about an assignment at school, ask him what the teacher could have done to make it a better learning experience, or, if your child wants to write a letter to the editor of a newspaper because bicycles aren't allowed on sidewalks, take a moment to have him think about other points of view—the elderly who may not see well, parents of small children, or homeowners liable for injuries on their property.

To tell you the truth, Tom, I read a book once and I quit smoking. I read a book and I got organized. I read a book and I made a quilt. Last week there was an article in the Wall Street Journal about entrepreneurs who began with a "How To" book. Why not a book about thinking?

Boni

Contracts

Because of the important role your literary agent will play in your eventual success, the contract you will sign with him or her is the most of your young writing career. There are only three types of agreements that one can enter into with a literary agent. Here they are, listed from the worst to the best.

A Time-Related Agreement

A time-related agreement basically states that any and all works that you compose will be the sole responsibility of a specific literary agent to market over a certain period of time, usually two years. Though this sort of agreement greatly benefits a literary agent, it is the worst possible contractual relationship that you can enter into. The reason is simple: you will be giving away all the representative rights of all your works for a significant period of time to an agency who you cannot guarantee is the best to handle your work. And if you have made a mistake in your decision to go with a certain agency, who pays most for the mistake? You do, via lost opportunities, in addition to having to potentially buy your way out of such an agreement if you do discover that the agent you chose is not the right one for you.

A Project-Related Agreement

Project-related agreements carry a significant amount of liability on your end as well, but not nearly as much as its time-related counterpart.

A project-related agreement states that you are allowing a literary agency to solely handle the representative rights to a specific project or projects. But what happens if the literary agent you signed on with under this sort of design doesn't turn out to be the right one for you? You may have to buy your way out of your agreement to take your project to another representative.

There is a way to make this sort of agreement more livable. Simply make sure it is stated in your contract that if your book project is not sold within a certain period of time (usually one year is very fair), for an acceptable amount, then you can choose to cancel your agreement with your literary agent at no cost. This will allow you to be able to go somewhere else without having to pay your former literary agent for any job he or she was unable to do.

Open-Ended Agreements

An open-ended contract is the best agreement that you can hope for, because it allows you to cancel your commitment with a literary agent at any time with no penalty to you. Varieties of this sort of agreement range from verbal agreements to typical written agreements.

Other Contractual Considerations

Expenses

If a literary agent charges you expenses outside of mailing costs, typing costs (if needed), and copying costs (if needed), they are probably getting some sort of kickback from the expenditures. Legitimate literary agents derive their incomes only from the commissions via sales of books. If literary agents have to charge for padded expenses, they're probably not doing their job. If that's the case, what does that tell you? Right. They're not very good salespeople, which is their primary function to you, and, thus, probably not the right literary agents for you or anyone else.

Hidden Costs

The bottom line is that if literary agents try to rope you into a contract that obligates you to pay for editing fees, rewriting fees, consultation fees, or anything like these, they're not worth your time. Again, like those who over-emphasize expenses, and probably severely pad them, they're probably not bringing in enough commission to support themselves and their business, so they turn to less honest means to acquire their income. Literary agents who hit you with hidden costs are not only not worth your time, but could prove to be extremely dangerous to your career. Avoid these people.

Deciding Upon a Literary Agent

If you are fortunate enough to have more than one literary agency offer you representation, which is what this entire system has been designed to do, think long and hard about which representative you choose to go with. Subscribe to publishermarketplace.com for at least one month and then go onto the agents' sites and check out even further the ones who are interested in you. Publishersmarketplace.com lists the majority of sales for agents for the past few years. See which publishers the agents who you are interested in are selling to and for how much are they selling the books they represent. Check out as well the number of books they have sold lately, within the last six months, and what types of books were sold.

Then call the agencies who have offered you contracts and ask them the following questions, along with any other queries you may have come up with on your own.

1. What number of publishers will they initially be submitting your work to? Getting the best deal from a traditional publisher means giving your book its best chance to succeed. The best way to guarantee that you are getting the best deal is to create a competition for it. To be able to do that, normally referred to by agents as an "auction," your representative needs to initially approach a minimum of a dozen publishers.

2. How soon will your material be in the hands of publishers? With this question you are gauging the degree of interest a perspective literary agent has in you and your material. If after having received the necessary material from you to approach publishers, it takes them longer than ten days to get it into the right hands, they are either not that interested or incompetent.

3. How long are they anticipating that it will take them to land an acceptable offer for you from a publisher? Six weeks for a nonfiction proposal package is good. Four to six months for a first novel is acceptable as well.

4. What type of dollar amount do they expect a publisher to be willing to risk on you and your book through an advance (and YES you should expect to receive an advance from a publisher–[the agent has 15% riding on this too, so he/she will demand an advance]if you don't expect one, how else would you expect to receive one?)? First of all, let me clarify that no agent, because of the subjectivity of the market, will be comfortable answering this question. Yet, it is still one you have to ask, for you need to know if what

they will be shooting for is in line with what the market bears. How do you know if that is that case? By this point, you should have already checked out publishersmarketplace.com and tracked the prices of money paid for books such as yours. Keep in mind that the upfront money you will be referring to is an advance, which, as mentioned previoulsy, translates to "risk money applied against royalties earned."

After you have asked all of your questions and concluded your interviews, decide whom you will be signing with. After you've made your decision and have properly informed your choice, contact your other final candidates, explaining what agency you went with and why. Make sure that you don't burn any bridges with the finalists whom you didn't choose. Make sure that the door is open to re-approach them in the future if, for some reason, your relationship with the agent you did chose doesn't work out.

Commonly Asked Questions About Submitting Your Writing

How long do you have to submit your submission package after getting a positive response from an agent?
It is of the utmost importance that your submission package be a good representation of both you and your idea. How long it will take to get it there is up to you. Simply inform your interested sources when you feel that you will be able to get your package to them. Unless yours is a very timely piece, and the chances are small that it will be, they are usually more than happy to work with you.

At the same time, it shows a significant amount of efficiency on your end if you politely keep them abreast of your progress on a monthly basis. It also doesn't allow them to lose you amongst the many writers who contact them on a daily, weekly, and monthly basis.

Should you have your material bound before submitting it?

The addition of a plastic spiral binding may seem to add an aura of professionalism to any submission. But it is not a necessity, nor is it expected by those who will be on the receiving end of your submission. In fact, there are some literary sources that detest spiral bindings because they make access to your work much harder for photocopying and distribution to their colleagues.

How long should a synopsis or proposal be?

Neither has any presupposed length. Each should simply and thoroughly introduce your idea, telling all that needs to be told, as gone over earlier, to fully enlighten your sources to the depth, scope, and potential of your project.

How much do you have to pay a literary agent?

If a literary agent charges you any more than a commission of between 10-15%, plus expecting you to reimburse them for reasonable out-of-pocket expenses (long distance costs, mailing expenses, and any typing or copying costs, if necessary), there's an excellent chance that you are dealing with a less–than-worthy source. In that case, stay clear of such people. Their inability to properly market books has probably led them to seek an income in less than honest ways.

What should I do when an agency asks to review my material on an exclusive basis?

Do not deceive an agency into thinking you are giving them an exclusive shot at your work when you're not. Just arrange your submission strategy to accommodate their request. Or even better, you can guarantee an agency asking for an exclusive look that you will not select any other agency for representation before hearing back from them, as long as they reply in a timely fashion of no more than three weeks after receipt.

Above all, it's important to be honest at all times.

Success Story by Dr. Tom Walker

From: Dr. Tom Walker, Gatlinburg, Tennessee
To: Tom Bird
Author: *The Force is With Us: The Conspiracy Against the supernatural, Spiritual and Paranormal*

Attached is a brief account of how, with your help, I got an agent, four offers, and signed a contract with Red Wheel/Weiser for release on their "A List" for April 2007.

Thanks to Tom's advice and business acumen, I have signed with a prominent East Coast literary agent and now have several publishers seriously considering my book. I'm not sure this would have been possible without Tom Bird. All I can say is that my decision to attend my first seminar with Tom, at the University of Tennessee a couple of years ago, was one of the very best choices I have ever made. And, from a practical point of view, it was the best monetary investment I have ever made. Keep up the excellent work, Tom!

The research on *The Force is With Us* began in November 1995. I completed the manuscript in November 2002, making it a very long seven-year journey. I worked on editing until the spring of 2004, at which time I took Tom's course at the University of Tennessee. Following his suggestions I contacted Jamie Saloff for formatting and Manjari Henderson for cover design, both of whom have become good friends. I self-published it in August 2004 using Lightning Source. People were very excited but sales were rather slow. Eventually I've sold or given review copies that have totalled about 1,000.

Query letters to agents proved uneventful. In one of Tom's newsletters he mentioned agent, Susan Lee Cohen. I asked Jamie if she thought Tom would mind me mentioning his name when I queried her by letter, and he agreed. I sent the letter along with a copy of my book. On the outside of the package I highlighted the phrase, "recommended by Tom Bird," and the first sentence of the query letter mentioned his name as well. I waited two months or so and heard nothing, so I made a call.

Susan answered and said she had the book but had not had a chance to review it. As we spoke she began flipping through it. Very soon remarks like, "fantastic," and "incredible" were spoken by her. She took it on vacation and she and a friend reviewed it in depth. Susan thought it was great, which made me feel good, to say the least! After a few weeks she signed me as her client. The contract was standard, but did state she wanted to represent me for all my works. This was the early summer of 2005.

Withing a few weeks review copies were going out. Approximately 30 or so were sent to publishers. In short order we had three interested: Quest, who I had spoken with at the BEA in New York City, Llewellyn, who I had also met at the Book Expo of America (BEA), and Red Wheel/Weiser. Most said the book was very impressive, but needed extensive editing, including Susan. Time-Warner sent it to commitee, but finally passed for the same reason. Atria, now an imprint of

Simon & Shuster, reluctantly passed. Earlier this year Cynthia Black of Atria called wanting it, only to be disappointed that I had signed with Red Wheel in late November 2005.

Jan Johnson of Red Wheel gave us the best offer, and they are personally editing it, something that began December 1, 2005 and is still continuing. Jan told Susan it has "blockbuster, mainstream potential," which made me feel great, particularly as I had written it with precisely that in mind. Althought I did not get the large advance I had hoped, I am happy with Red Wheel. It is of interest that I signed the contract with Red Wheel on November 25, 2005, ten years to the day I began the project. They also want first crack at my next book, which I've already completed.

Jan is one the of top editors in the world with "mind, body, spirit books" and they are very excited about *The Force is With Us*, and are commited to marketing it and helping me promote it. It is being released on their "A List" in early April 2007 and will be marketed worldwide. In January of this year Susan said via email she was getting "lots of foreign interest, so it should sell well around the world." In the meantime I'm waiting . . . and excited!

I credit Tom Bird with much of this success. As a first-time author, Tom taught me his method of self-publishing, which I followed to the letter. He also directly helped in getting my agent, who in fact had been his former agent. His friend Jamie Saloff has been a great help as well. Thanks for everything, Tom. I'm looking forward to the release of *The Force is With Us* next year.

Law #7

Trust your literary agent and treat him/her with respect.

HAVING LANDED THE REPRESENTATION OF A WELL-KNOWN literary agent and having your book taken to the marketplace is a very exciting event, but the work doesn't stop there. There are still three basic activities you are responsible for during this step.

First, the great excitement and exhilaration of this phase, if not properly channeled, could lead to rampant confusion, doubt, and frustration. The confusion and doubt come in response to your great success and fortune. Yes, there is a downside. In most cases, we have a difficult time believing that what is happening to us, that which we wanted for so long, has appeared at all, let alone so fast. As a result, doubts start to dominate our minds.

I haven't heard from my agent today. I wonder if all is going well? Maybe all the publishing houses that my book was sent to turned us down. Yeah, and maybe he's (or she's) just frightened to tell me. Maybe I had better give him (or her) a call.

Hey, I've got a great idea that I think will make my

book even more marketable. I know the stuff is already out to the publishing houses, but I think that I'll give my agent a call anyway.

Hmmmm, let's see, what reason could I use today to give my agent a call? I don't want to be a pain in the butt, so I had better think of something. I mean, I don't want to call and just bug him (or her) about the book. Let's see, what excuse did I use yesterday, because I don't want to use the same one today? Oh yeah, I remember now. Well, maybe today I'll use the one about the chocolate cake I know he (or she) likes. I'm quite a cook and I could...

My agent) said he (or she) would have my book sold by today. Or at least I think that's what he (or she) said. Well, it's not sold, damn it. I think it's about time that I call and give that son of a gun a piece of my mind. I'm not going to be seconded to any client. I don't care who it is. I'll show this son of a gun who he (or she) is dealing with. He's (or she's) going to get a piece of my mind. Probably just needs a good kick in the butt. Well, I'll show him (her).

I know that it's after midnight, but I just can't sleep. This whole sale thing is just driving me crazy. I need to be reassured. I'm sure that my agent won't mind if I call. That's why he (or she) gave me his (or her) home number anyway, isn't it?

I'm sure you get the idea. No matter how refined you are in most circumstances, because of the impact of this sort of arrangement and situation, there's an excellent chance that you may become unwound, and in doing so, you could ruin and then dissolve the valuable relationship that you waited so long for and worked so hard to acquire.

To prevent yourself from experiencing this form of self-sabotage, I strongly suggest that you set up some sort of communicative routine with your agent where he or she checks in with you via phone, e-mail, or fax every 3-4 weeks, and then stick to it. Don't let your fears, worries, doubts, and concerns get the better of you. Using the above technique, you will be receiving the timely updates you deserve, while you'll be giving your agent the time, space, trust, and freedom that he or she needs to do the job.

> *The information that Tom Bird provides instills confidence and is empowering.*
> *Mark Atkins, 'Be Strong for Me' (Dove Books)*

Employing a system such as this and sticking to it will pay off for you in spades. Your agent will appreciate your professionalism and will reward you by being able to devote more of his or her energy to the sale of your work. Your sane and professional approach will also make you stand out favorably from the other clients that he or she represents. As a result, you will get better service all the way around, and he or she will be able to boast about you to the potential purchasers of your work as a model client, which goes very, very far in today's high-stress, crazy, emotional world of publishing.

Second, use the time while your work is being shopped to study the following material on publishing agreements. By doing so, not only will you be preparing yourself to understand and then make the proper decisions when your contract comes through, but you will be sending out good vibes to yourself, as well.

Third, and probably the most important step that you can take to benefit yourself, your agent, and the eventual elevation of your goals as a writer, is to begin on a second book. I know that your logical mind is probably telling you that doing so is crazy. "I mean, shouldn't I wait until the first one is sold before I go wasting time on working on another one?"

No. Go ahead and start work on that next project now. You'll have to just take my advice here. But, toss the following back at your old logical mind to see if these rock-solid reasons for doing so will better ease its concerns.

The first reason that you begin work on a second project is in hopes that you will become so distracted with it that you will better be able to give your agent the time, space, and freedom he or she needs to best complete the sale of your work.

Also, your second book will be better than your first and, as a result, may have a better chance of selling. In fact, in my estimation, my students' second works are usually at least three times as well written as their first works. The reason for this is because so much time and energy is expended learning to write about your first book that there is little time left to address the actual inspiration as it comes through you. That reverses with your work on the second book, which can't help but make your work a more powerful read.

Third, you begin work on your second book at this time because you're a writer and writers write. We're not professional telephone watchers who just sit around waiting for our agents to call, even though you may be hard pressed to find an agent that would agree with me on that point.

Another reason to begin work on your second book is because you're probably already in good writing shape, and you might as well take advantage of it.

The final reason for doing so is because having a second or third or whatever project ready to go to market just provides you with that many more opportunities to succeed. Remember the primary point in this section, though. Make yourself different. Make yourself special. Conduct yourself professionally, and you'll be amazed at the results.

In this industry, the squeaky wheel doesn't get greased, it gets replaced if it squeaks too often, especially if it is a brand new wheel.

Commonly Asked Questions

How long will it take for my book to be sold?

That all depends on several factors (the aggressiveness and knowledge of your literary agent, the quality of your material, the mindset of the publishing industry at the time of your submission), most of which are out of your control.

The best way to answer this question for yourself is to ask your literary agent's opinion on how long it will take your material to be sold. Do this before you sign a contract with him or her, and this will help you gauge how aggressive they plan to be.

How much can I expect to make on my first book?

That varies greatly depending upon the above factors and the type of material that you are writing. However, when books of all types are taken into consideration, the average advance for the first-time author in hardcover usually works out to around $10,000, coupled with the standard royalty rates of 10% on the first 5,000 copies sold; 12-1/2% on the second 5,000; and 15% on any books sold over 10,000. But it has been my experience that writers using this system usually receive twice the average advance for their fiction and over three times as much for their non-fiction.

Should I use a pen name?

The name that you choose to put on the cover of your work is totally up to you. Though, the only time it is really necessary to use a pen name is when you deliberately want to hide your affiliation with a project because a similar book or two by you will be available soon, such as in the case of a romance author releasing two new works at the same time.

How beneficial are writing groups?

Because they are usually run by well-meaning but unsuccessful writers, most groups of this sort do more to hurt than to help you. If you can find a group that is headed by a successful, knowledgeable, and egoless published writer with a proven system to share, you will probably have found a fertile place to learn, grow, and succeed. If not, there are plenty of books on the shelves that would help you much more than the typical writers group, which often does more to bring you down than lift you up.

How long will it take for me to get published?

The answer to that question is completely subjective and depends totally on you. However, if you move swiftly and confidently, you should be able to breeze through the first two steps in one to two months for the shorter pieces and four to six months for books. How long the process will take from there depends upon the aforementioned factors.

Can I really make a living doing this?

Definitely! In fact, with the ever-expanding media markets, there has never been a better time to be a writer than today. Also, writing is one of those rare professions that doesn't place any weight on your age, gender, sexual preference, education, color, or socioeconomic background. If you can write, want to write, and are willing to endure the emotional upheavals you may put yourself through with the submission of your work, you have what it takes to make it in this business.

How much money will it take for me to become an author?

Money isn't much of a factor here. Sure, you should have a computer, and it's a good idea if you take a class or two. Then there are costs for mailing and paper and such. But outside of that, writers pay for their successes with the sweat of their souls. The monetary investment is small, but the emotional output is great.

Law #8

**When signing a contract with a
traditional book publisher, always make sure
you know what it is you are signing.**

A S SPECIFIED MUCH EARLIER IN THIS BOOK, THERE ARE SOME
primary components of a publishing agreement that
you should be aware of.

Remember, you are ultimately responsible for any
contract you sign. So, it's best to fully understand all of the
necessary elements of that contract before doing so. It's
not fair to either you or your agent if you leave up to him
or her the decisions that will affect you and your career so
deeply.

An Advance Against Royalties Earned

As has been defined previously, an advance against
royalties earned is more commonly referred to just as an
advance, and is defined as risk money against potential
royalties earned. It is what your publisher hopefully will
be offering you. It is the dollar figure authors continually
refer to when they talk about how much money they have
received for their books.

Payment of an Advance

Though they can take almost any form, advances are either paid in two or three payments. If paid in two payments, half of the advance is usually given upon the signing of a book contract, and the second half is received after the manuscript has been delivered. On the three-payment system, one-third is received upon the signing of an agreement; the second third is sent out after the first half of the manuscript has been delivered; and the last third is paid once the remainder of the manuscript has been completed.

Royalties

As covered previously, royalties are paid in two ways. First, they can be paid upon the actual cash received by the publisher, which can be anywhere from a 35-55% discount off the cover price of the book. Or secondly, they can be paid on the actual list price of the book, a vast difference. Obviously, the latter alternative will earn you significantly more than the former.

Deadline

This is the consideration that most new writers innocently squirm over most. But don't allow yourself to fret over being able to make your deadline. Publishers usually deal very fairly in this regard. They certainly are not the browbeaters that unknowing writers and a misled public make them out to be. A publisher usually discusses with you when they would ideally like a book completed and are very open to your realistic abilities.

Copyright

The publisher handles for you the copyrighting of your manuscript in your name.

Paperback Considerations

If your publisher sells the paperback rights for your hardback book to another publishing house, they are entitled to a percentage of anything you make from the softcover sale of your book. If they publish your paperback edition in-house, they receive no extra percentages or fees, and you receive your agreed upon royalty rate.

Book Club Rights

If your publishing house sells the rights of your work to a book club, they receive a percentage of all monies you earn.

Subsidiary Rights

As with the two categories listed directly above, your publishing house receives a percentage of all monies earned from the sale of subsidiary rights. For example, if your publisher sells a first serial excerpt of your book to a major magazine, which pays $20,000 for the piece, you will receive a $10,000 check, minus your agent's fee, based upon a 50-50 split.

Foreign Rights

If your publishing house sells the foreign rights to your work to another firm, it is standard that you will be expected to turn over a percentage of the monies earned from your foreign sales to your publisher. If the house you contract with publishes your book in-house for foreign consumption, you will not be expected to share a high percentage of all monies you earn with your publisher. In such a case, you will typically receive a standard royalty rate.

Movie Rights

Since most publishing houses do not specialize either in the sale or production of movies, it is in the best interests of you and your literary representative to retain these rights.

> *I am delighted to tell you that "Fractal Murders" has been honored by being listed on the Fall Book Scene Mystery Top Ten list. This is a great honor as selections are made based on nominations from independent bookstores nationwide.*
> *Mark Cohen, U.S.A.*

Law #9

**For articles and short stories,
submit your query letters
direct to publications.**

SINCE MOST LITERARY AGENTS DO NOT REPRESENT ARTICLES, short stories, and poetry, it is common practice to submit your Query Letter Package directly to the editor of a publication unless the magazine, or whomever you are approaching, has on staff a submissions or acquisitions editor or a specialty editor who would be in charge of reviewing your type of material.

When you have an article or short story you want to publish, always submit your query letter directly to publications you feel may be interested; do not go through a literary agent. Literary agents are not usually the best sources for the sale of shorter material. They prefer to concentrate on books, which is where the bigger money is.

Querying Magazine Articles, Short Stories, and Poetry

Finding Sources

Where can you find a listing of sources that you can approach with your ideas for a magazine article or short story? Here are a few suggestions:

- Newsstand: This is the best place to go when researching sources for your article and short story ideas. Not only can you catch a glimpse of the publication or publications you will be approaching, but you can also copy down the correct name and address of the appropriate contact in each case. In a business with a high turnover rate like the magazine field, this is a necessity.

- *Writer's Digest* by Writer's Digest Books: This publication boasts hundreds of potential sources for your work. However, because of the high turnover referred to above, oftentimes your potential editors may have left for another position, the magazine may have gone out of business, or the publication could have completely changed focus, making any possible submission a sure reject. That's why the newsstand approach is such a strongly suggested mode of gathering sources. Using that technique, your information will always be in its most present, up-to-date form.

- *The Writer's Handbook* by The Writer Inc.: This publication provides a smaller listing than its competitor listed directly above, with many of the same drawbacks.

Submitting Queries for Magazine Articles, Short Stories, or Poetry

As with books, it is essential that you utilize a multiple submissions system. First, arrange your potential sources from who would pay you the most for a prospective piece to who would pay you the least. If you don't know what a specific publication would pay you, call and ask them, or use a SASE and send for a copy of their writer's guidelines or visit their websites. Calling is quicker, but occasionally you may find yourself caught in an awkward position by doing so.

After you've properly arranged your sources, send to the few top-paying sources first, giving them at least four weeks to respond. Then send to the next highest paying group, allowing them the same amount of time to reply, before approaching your remaining sources.

Why do you go to your best paying sources first? The answer is simple. You want to allow those sources that can offer you the most money, as well as the highest degree of exposure (the two usually go hand in hand), the first opportunity to publish your work. By starting at the bottom, you may be selling yourself short by potentially keeping your work from being published by a much better paying source.

A Special Note on Poetry

If you are sending off a Query Letter Package to approach potential sources about a book of poetry, follow the design described above for a non-fiction Query Letter Package.

Commonly Asked Questions About Query Submissions

What about those sources that accept completed works? Should I still query them?

Yes. By always sending your Query Letter Package first, you will be able to acquire important preliminary information concerning your source's reaction to your ideas. Following this procedure will afford you the opportunity to modify and appropriately adjust your work before submitting it for review. Thus, always sending your Query Letter Package first will increase your chance of an eventual sale.

Should we write to or adjust to a specific market?

Write what you feel most comfortable writing, no matter what genre or area of writing that may be. That's the only way that you will be able to continue to write and, thus, succeed. Learn from your mistakes and adjust to the specific requirements of individual markets, but don't compromise by writing something that you have no desire to be associated with. Write what is in your heart and to the market that is most suitable for your form of expression. Compromising yourself leads you away from the areas in which you will write best, and, thus, deters your efforts toward publication.

Should query letters be sent out before a project is complete?

If you do not have a completed manuscript, I suggest you employ the methods I share in my book *Your Artist Within*, which will enable you to complete your book in thirty days or less. Then, send out your Query Letter Package. However, having a completed manuscript in hand before sending out your query is not a necessity, even though it does work to your advantage.

What if I've already completed a manuscript?

Bravo! To have already completed a manuscript without gathering the necessary confirmations one gets from a Query Letter Package says a lot of great things about you.The drawback is that it will make your query letter a little more difficult to write (you'll probably feel as if you're being asked to shrink your entire book into one page), but just follow the same procedures that I outlined earlier, then be ready to make whatever changes are necessary to your manuscript before submitting it.

How do I protect my work from being stolen?

Before I begin to address how to protect your work, it is important for you to understand that you cannot copy-right an idea. This means that if you submit a Query Letter Package for review, you can only copyright the Query Letter Package and not the idea that it represents.

So, what do you do? Simple. Though it is my opinion that work is very rarely stolen within this business (the risks are just too high), it is very simple to protect anything that you've written.

You yourself copyright your book, or with the assistance of an attorney, through the Library of Congress. Doing it yourself will cost you around $45. All you have to do is contact the Library of Congress in Washington, D.C. (via their website www.copyright.gov/register) to get all the appropriate registration forms. Of course, if you go through an attorney, you will have to pay legal fees to get your copyright.

How long do I have before replying to a request for my material?

Don't be scared if you receive an acceptance before you have even started working on a project. You'll have plenty of time, usually up to six months or so, to get back to any interested parties with material. The only thing to keep in mind is that you don't want to let potential sources forget who you are while they are waiting. So give them a call or drop them a line every now and again just to update them on your progress.

Law #10

Get all of the agreed-upon contractual arrangements with a magazine and/or newspaper in writing before submitting your work.

I N GETTING ALL OF THE AGREED-UPON CONTRACTUAL arrangements with a magazine and/or newspaper in writing before submitting your work, there are three ways in which to do so:

1. Via the use of a written, legal contract. If you plan to do a lot of this work, it would be to your advantage to have your attorney draw up a simple agreement that you could adapt to the specifics of your situation.

2. By a confirming letter, listing all the specifics agreed upon, sent by you to your source, which your source acknowledges with his or her signature at the bottom of the correspondence and then returns to you.

Elements of a Magazine Contract

The following are the elements that need to be agreed upon in a magazine/newspaper contract.

Money

With the exception of well-known magazines with substantial circulations that offer a very rewarding standard fee to their writers, how much you will be paid is determined by a few factors: the size and budget of the publication you are dealing with, how badly they may want your piece, your credentials, and, most of all, your confidence when negotiating your fee.

Basically, a publication with a tight budget will offer you the least amount of money they feel that you will accept to write a piece. So don't be afraid to say "No" to their first offer. In fact, in dealing with such publications, it's not a bad negotiating practice to routinely say "No" to each offer you receive until you can receive an offer that is fair.

Whether You Will Be Writing on Assignment or Speculation

Writing on speculation simply means that a magazine will agree to pay you only after seeing a completed piece and accepting it for publication. If they like it, you'll get paid what you agreed upon. If not, maybe they'll give you another chance to do it over. But maybe they won't.

Writing on assignment means that a publication will commit to your piece without seeing it first, though this luxury is usually reserved for the proven writer.

Kill Fee

A kill fee is a specific percentage of the money a publication has agreed to pay you for a piece if, for some reason, your work is not published by an agreed-upon date. I usually agree to nothing lower than a 50% kill fee. This means if I sell an article for $1,000, and the magazine that I contracted with doesn't run my article by a specific date, I will be paid $500 for the piece and its rights will be returned to me.

Payment Schedule

In the world of magazines, there are only two ways that you are paid, either on acceptance or upon publication. Of course, being paid once your material is accepted is always best. But that right is often reserved only for the seasoned or experienced writer. Being paid upon publication means that you won't be issued a check until after your work appears in print, which means that you may not see any money until months after you've finished writing a piece.

Expenses

Make sure to discuss being reimbursed for any out-of-pocket expenses you may run into when working on a piece. This is an area that many writers sorely neglect, and, thus, they net a lot less on their writing than they could have.

Photographs

Oftentimes publications are unwilling to pay the rates of a freelance photographer, so often a deal hinges on whether you, the writer, are capable of providing accompanying photographs. Make sure to negotiate an additional fee up-front before doing so. In almost every case, you will be paid well.

Length

The agreed-upon length of a piece determines how severely a magazine can alter your work without your permission. For example, let's say that you agreed to write a 2,000-word article and just before your publication date an aggressive salesperson at the magazine makes a last-minute sale for some advertising space. The magazine would love to chop out 300 words of your article to make room for the ad, but they can't unless they consult you first. Of course, if you didn't have this clause in your agreement, they could chop all they wanted, literally mutilating your work. Who would look bad? You. Your name is on the article. The proper inclusion of this clause prohibits that nightmare from happening.

Delivery

This area of any contract simply states the date you will send your piece to a magazine.

Publication Date

Agreeing upon exactly when your piece will be published keeps a magazine from procrastinating in regards to printing your piece. It also ensures that you will be paid at an agreed-upon time and guarantees your material can be sold elsewhere if the magazine you've contracted with doesn't publish your work by the prede-termined date.

Rights

There are three types of rights that you need to consider when negotiating the placement of a piece. The first type is First North American Rights, which allows a publication to print your piece before anyone else in the country. That's it. After that, the rights revert back to you, and you can do what you please with the material.

The second type of rights are Resale Rights. These are utilized only after you have already sold your First North American Rights. As I'm sure you would expect, resale rights are usually less valuable than First North American Rights.

The third type involves the selling of Exclusive or All Rights to a publication. This means that they can do what they want with the piece. If they sell it for use somewhere else, it's OK, as long as they give you your byline.

Of course, if you involve yourself in this third type of situation and sell All Rights, you should be compensated even better than you would have been for the sale of your First North American Rights. Usually, a writer is compensated up to four times as much as he or she would have received for his or her First North American Rights, or is paid a percentage, anywhere between 50-75%, of any further monies earned from the eventual sale of the piece.

Just remember: In dealing with a magazine, always get any deal in writing and never start writing until your signed, written agreement has been received.

Two sample agreements follow.

Informal Magazine Agreement

January 4, 2006
Mike Mason
1234 Anystreet
Westport, Michigan 97863
123-321-1234

Roger Wright, Editor
Airline Magazine
1222 Blvd. of the Americas
New York, New York 10010

Dear Roger,

It is with great pleasure that I write this letter in regard to Airline Magazines commissioning of my piece entitled Above The Rest. As we discussed on the 27th of last month, I am confirming that I will be producing the 2,000-word article on a speculation basis and will have the work to you no later than April 5, 2006.

If the work meets with your satisfaction, a decision will reach me no later than April 30, 2004. I will be paid $750 for the First North American Rights of the article, plus any incidental expenses such as mailing costs, long-distance costs, etc.

As well, we agreed that I will be paid upon publication of the work, which is scheduled for no later than your December issue of this year. If for some reason, after accepting the material, you cannot use it by that time, I will still be paid a 50% kill fee, and the First North American Rights will revert back to me.

In addition, as per your request, I will be more than happy to provide the accompanying photos for the article. As you requested, I will provide you with several digital photographs by April 30, 2006. Your magazine will be responsible for the processing and developing of the film. If my article is accepted, I will not only be reimbursed for the cost of the film, but paid $150 for each photo that I took which is used in your magazine. If you choose not to use my article, I will still be reimbursed for the cost of the film, all the negatives and accompanying photos will be returned to me, and I am free to sell their First North American Rights elsewhere.

This concludes all that we agreed upon. All rights not herein granted are reserved to me, and this letter when signed by both of us will constitute our agreement. Any amendments to it must be made in writing and agreed upon by both of us.

Sincerely,

_____

Mike Mason

_____

Roger Wright

Sample Formal Magazine Agreement

AGREEMENT

This agreement made as of the _____ of _____, _____, by and between _____ of _____, _____(hereinafter referred to as AUTHOR), and _____ of _____ Magazine (hereinafter referred to as MAGAZINE).

WHEREAS, the AUTHOR agreed to provide on speculation, for the purpose of a First North American Rights publication, a _____ word article, currently titled _____ _____, to MAGAZINE by _____, _____.

THE MAGAZINE agrees to review the AUTHOR'S submission as quickly as possible and contact the AUTHOR with a final decision in regards to publication no later than _____. If, at that time, the MAGAZINE decides not to publish the AUTHOR'S work, then the MAGAZINE shall return all copies of the above to the AUTHOR within ten (10) working days, and all rights will revert immediately to the AUTHOR.

IF, HOWEVER, THE MAGAZINE AGREES TO PUBLISH THE AUTHOR'S WORK, the AUTHOR will be paid $800, plus any expenses up to $200, for the article within thirty (30) days of the MAGAZINE'S publication of the above. As well, the AUTHOR agrees to provide several digital photographs on the above topic to the MAGAZINE by _____, _____, for which the AUTHOR will be paid

_____ apiece for any of AUTHORs photographs that are published by the MAGAZINE.

AS WELL, the MAGAZINE agrees to publish the AUTHOR'S article no later than _____, _____. If for whatever reason after accepting the AUTHOR's article by _____, _____, then the AUTHOR shall be paid a kill fee of 50%, be reimbursed for all out-of-pocket expenses, and all copies of the AUTHOR's work shall be returned to him within ten (10) working days from the date listed above in this paragraph and all rights to the above shall return to the AUTHOR.

THIS AGREEMENT, which constitutes the entire understanding of the parties, may be amended or modified only in writing signed by both parties, and shall be governed by the laws of the Commonwealth of _____.

IN WITNESS WHEREOF, the parties hereunto have set their respective hands and seals as of the day and year first above written.

_____
WITNESS:

_____
AUTHOR

_____
WITNESS:

_____
MAGAZINE

Law #11

Listen.

LISTEN. THAT'S RIGHT. LISTEN. FOR IF YOU LISTEN, YOU will learn. If you learn, you will understand; if you understand, you will grow; and if you grow, you will succeed. But it all begins with LISTENING.

The people you will be listening to are your prospective literary agents, editors and publishers. These people might offer you suggestions. But they will only do so if they see potential in you and your work, and their comments will help you reach that potential. That doesn't mean you should take their advice verbatim, but you would be missing a huge opportunity to grow and succeed faster if you were not to LISTEN. Whatever you do with their suggestions is up to you. But LISTEN, for this industry will teach you everything that you need to learn if you just do that.

Why wouldn't you LISTEN in the first place?

Because all of us have been hurt at one time or another during our lives in response to creatively expressing ourselves. The greater the amount of time between when that initial blow took place and now, the greater the defensiveness on our end. It's that defensiveness that could keep us from hearing what could benefit us the most. Don't allow that to happen to you. Shrug off the past, close your mouth, open your ears, and LISTEN. If you are asked to take into consideration some suggestions to improve your work, and you agree with them, then do it. That doesn't mean that you have to adhere to anything. But LISTEN. You may just learn something that will greatly contribute to the speed and breadth of your eventual success.

Losers visualize the penalties of failure. Winners visualize the rewards of success.

Dr. Rob Gilbert

You'll never be the same after embarking on your writing career. You'll just keep getting better and better at publishing and happier and happier as you go.

This above all else is the most important law of publishing. Listen first to the Source of your inspiration as a writer and then listen to all of the messengers. They will lead you to where it is that your soul is calling you to go, proving to you that you were born to be published. I promise.

About the Author

A Quick History of
The Tom Bird Method™

TWENTY-FOUR YEARS AGO TOM BIRD WAS A PUBLICIST WITH the Pittsburgh Pirates. However, like so many in the world, at heart he was a writer.

Tom had tried every orthodox method possible to become the successful author he felt himself to be, but nothing had worked. Not willing to believe he had been blessed with a dream, but without a way to live it, Tom developed his own system for both writing and publishing. This system is now referred to as *The Tom Bird Method*™.

Within four weeks of employing his method, Tom landed a literary agent who, at the time, was the most renowned in publishing history. Six weeks later, Tom's first book was sold to Harper & Row, then the third largest publisher in the world, for a price equivalent to three times Tom's annual salary with the Pirates. This enabled him to resign from his position and write full-time.

Shortly after Tom's first book was released, his phone was overwhelmed with calls from aspiring authors wondering how someone so young as he had done it. Tom responded to their queries by offering a series of classes at local Pittsburgh colleges and universities. Soon, word spread of the simple, direct. and effective methods he taught, creating nationwide demand.

Over the last quarter of a century, Tom has remained committed to sharing his method with writers all across the globe. He has made over 3000 lecture appearances before more than 50,000 students at over 110 different campuses.

Just a few of the colleges and universities which Tom has appeared at are Duke, William and Mary, Temple, Ohio State, Penn State, University of North Carolina, University of Florida, University of Arizona, University of Texas, and Emory University.

Tom has authored sixteen books and has articles in over fifty different publications.

His books are:

Willie Stargell co-authored with Willie Stargell (Harper & Row, 1984)

Tom Bird's Selective Guide to Literary Agents (Sojourn, 1985)

How to Get Published (Sojourn, 1986)

KnuckleBALLS co-authored with Phil Niekro (Freundlich Books, 1986)

Literary Law (Sojourn, 1986)

Beyond Words (Sojourn, 1987)

POWs of WWII: Forgotten Men Tell Their Stories (Praeger, 1990)

Fifty-Two Weeks or Less to the Completion of Your First Book (Sojourn, 1990)

The Author's Den, An Interactive Computer Program (Sojourn, 1993)

Hawk co-authored with Andre Dawson (Zondervan, 1994)

Hawk the Children's Version (Zondervan, 1995)

Get Published Now! (Sojourn, 2001)

The Spirit of Publishing (Sojourn, 2003)

Releasing Your Artist Within (Sojourn, 2004)

You Were Born to. . . Write (Sojourn, 2006)

The list of periodicals which have published Tom's work is extensive. *Parade, USA Today, Popular Mechanics,* and *The Pittsburgh Post-Gazette* are but a few of them.

Tom also hosts intensive retreats, including one on book publicity and promotion. As a publicist, Tom's career began in 1979, when he was hired by the Pittsburgh Pirates. They captured the World Series that year, affording Tom with a wealth of hands-on experience with the media.

Over his next three seasons, Tom served as the team's official spokesperson. He held press conferences, scheduled talk show appearances, supervised publicity campaigns and addressed the requests of small market media, major magazines and newspapers, and television networks.

Tom transferred his expertise in publicity to his career in publishing when his first book was released by Harper & Row in 1984. He handled the publicity tours of his next three books as well.

Over the last twenty-two years, he has utilized his publicity expertise to sell more than 98,000 copies of his self-published books.

> *Tom's charismatic personality and zest make him a natural for any type of media appearance, no matter who the audience."*
>
> Susan Harrow, marketing and media coach and author of "Sell Yourself Without Selling Your Soul" (Harper Resource, 2002).

As with the number of periodicals which have published work written by Tom, the number of publications which have featured articles on Tom is far-reaching. *The Los Angeles Times, Toronto Sun, Atlanta Journal-Constitution,* and *San Francisco Chronicle* have all featured articles about Tom or his work. Newspapers and periodicals in nearly all the major cities in the US have covered him, including *The Washington Post, Chicago Sun Times, Boston Globe* and *Herald, New York Times,* and *Miami Herald.*

The same goes for television and radio shows, and/or stations which have featured either Tom or his work. A handful of them include *The David Letterman Show, The Tonight Show, The Today Show, CBS Morning News,* and *The Charlie Rose Show.*

Tom was born and raised in Erie, Pennsylvania, and now lives in Sedona, Arizona with his partner, Tammy, and their daughter, Skyla. They share their home with two dogs, Rikka and Jada, five cats, and two birds.

Tom's interests include yoga, eating vegan, hiking, basketball, football, baseball, climbing, camping, racquetball, working out, playing cards and reading.

Appendix A
A Checklist of Self-Publishing

Step One, Your Business Foundation:

Form a Corporation

Acquire an Employer Identification Number

Acquire a Sales Tax/State Business License

Acquire City Business License

Acquire a Lightning Source Account

Step Two, Your Book:

Write Book

Choose Size

Decide on Price

Choose Cover Designer

Choose Text Formatter for Layout and Design

Choose Potential Text Editor

Choose Potential Style Editor

Put Together Illustrations, Gather Photographs

Write Extraneous Information:

    Author's Bio

    Acknowledgments

    Dedication

    Contact Page

    Order Page

    Teaser

Acquire Accolades/Endorsements

Get Permission Slips for Endorsements Signed

Step Three, Protecting Your Product:

Consider Acquiring a Trademark _____

Acquire Trademark Verification from an Attorney _____

Acquire a Copyright – Library of Congress; Text: $30.00 _____

Acquire a Copyright – Library of Congress; Cover: $30.00 _____

Acquire a Copyright – LOC; published book: Form TX w/in 3 months of printing – 2 copies of book plus $30.00 _____

Acquire Library of Congress – Pre-assigned control number (PCN); www.loc.gov _____

Acquire Library of Congress Cataloging in Publication Division (CIP); Send book. (You are only eligible to participate in the CIP program after you have published three books.) _____

Acquire Bowker International Standard Business Number (ISBN); www.bowkerlink.com _____

Acquire Bowker Registration; www.bowkerlink.com _____

Step Four, Promotion:

Construct a Media/News Kit _____

Collect Testimonials _____

Write Interview Questions _____

Write Press Release _____

Choose Excerpt from Book _____

Construct a Sample Flyer _____

Write a News/Press Release _____

Design Promotional Bookmarks as Handouts _____

Design a Business Card _____

Design Stationery

Design a Website

Join the Publishers Marketing Association; www.pma-online.org

Join the American Association of Publishers

Join the American Booksellers Association; www.bookweb.org

ABA BookBuyer's Handbook; www.bookweb.com

List with the Contemporary Authors; www.galegroup.com

List in International Directory of Little Mag & Small Press; www.dustbooks.com

List in the Literary Marketplace; www.literarymarketplace.com

List in the Publishers Directory; www.galegroup.com

List in the Small Press Record of Books In Print (also International Dir.); www.dustbooks.com

List in Bowker Books In Print; www.bowkers.com

Enhance Listing on Amazon.com; www.amazon.com

Enhance Listing on Barnes & Noble; www.barnesandnoble.com

Enhance Listing on Books a Million; www.booksamillion.com

List on www.seekbooks.com

List on www.elgrande.com

Reviews:

Publishers Weekly; www.publishersweekly.com/abput/forecast-guidelines.asp

Library Journal; Send Galley or Book; www.libraryjournal.com/about/submission.asp

Kirkus Reviews; www.kirkusreviews.com

Booklist (American Library Association); www.ala.org

New York Times Book Review; www.nytimes.com/books

LA Times Book Review; www.latimes.com

Forward Magazine; www.forwardmagazine.com

Baker & Taylor; www.btol.com

Booklist (American Library Assoc.); www.ala.org/booklist

Chicago Tribune Books; www.chicagotribune.com/leisure/books

Ruminator Review; www.ruminator.com

H. W. Wilson Co.; www.hwwilson.com

Independent Publisher; www.bookpublishing.com

Ingram Book Group; www.ingrambookgroup.com

Kirkus Reviews; www.kirkusreviews.com

Library Journal; www.libraryjournal.com

Library of Congress Acquisitions; www.loc.gov

Library of Congress CIP; www.loc.gov

Los Angeles Times Book Review; www.latimes.com

Midwest Book Review; www.execpc.com/~mbr/bookwatch

Newsday; www.newsday.com

New York Review of Books; www.nybooks.com

New York Times (send out first); www.nytimes.com/books

Publishers Weekly; www.publishersweekly.com

Rainbo Electronic Reviews; www.rainboreviews.com

Reader's Digest Select Editions; www.readersdigest.com

San Francisco Chronicle; www.sfgate.com/eguide/books

Small Press Review; www.dustbooks.com

USA Today; www.usatoday.com

Voice Literary Supplement; www.villagevoice.com

Washington Post (send out first); www.washingtonpost.com

Book Clubs:

www.literarymarketplace.com

Book-of-the-Month Club; www.bookspan.com

Doubleday Select; www.booksonline.com

Literary Guild; www.literaryguild.com

Writer's Digest Book Club; www.writersdigest.com

Other:

Contact Radio/TV Talk Shows

Design Author Promotion Tour

Schedule Autograph Parties

Schedule Speaking Engagements

Schedule Book Fairs

Schedule Book Expo America (May); www.bookexpo.com

Potentially Schedule Frankfurt Book Fair (October);
www.frankfurt-book-fair.com

Pre-Publication Review Mailing

Documents included in the Pre-Publication Review Mailing sent 4 to 5 months prior to publish date:

Cover letter
Bound Galley with Book Review Slip as cover (sample enclosed)
News Release
Author Bio including a section listing Future Books By TheAuthor
Fax Response Transmittal Sheet (sample enclosed – you may want
  to change the name, etc.)
SASE addressed to the publisher (the cover letter requested a clip
  ping/tear sheet of the review)

Post-Publication Review Mailing

Documents included in the Post-Publication Review Mailing:

Cover letter
Published Book
Review Slip included as an informational 8.5 x 11 sheet (sample
  enclosed)
ABI Form copy
4" x 6" or larger, photo of book cover
Flyer/brochure
Testimonials
News Release
Author Bio
Expanded informational sheet explaining the question – What
  makes _____ (name of book) unique?
Expanded informational sheet explaining – Who is the audience
  for _____ (name of book)?
Fax Response Transmittal Sheet (sample enclosed – you may want
  to change the name, etc.)
SASE addressed to the publisher (the cover letter requested a clip
  ping/tear sheet of the review)

I used a professional border around all of the documents included
in this mailing.

SETS

Spiritually Enlightening Thoughts™
Teaching Children How To Connect With God
Shirley Hildreth

Category : (**BISG Major subjects**)	Religion (adult)/Family and Relationships/Self-Help
Edition:	First Edition
Specifications:	Soft cover; 7" x 9"; 128 pages; illustrated
Season:	Winter, 2003
Price:	$19.95
ISBN No.:	0-9740500-0-8
LOC Control No.:	2003094617
Intended Audience:	Parents, clergy and teachers of children in a religious setting, extended family members, psychologists, and caregivers of children.
Promotional Plans:	Author tour, space advertising, direct mail, writer's conferences
Distribution:	Ingram Book Group
Trademarks:	SETS: Spiritually Enlightening Thoughts and Muse Imagery are trademarks of Muse Imagery LLC, a Nevada Limited Liability Co.

Description:

SETS Teaching Children To Connect With God is a book about a teaching method called Spiritually Enlightening Thoughts (SETS)™ and builds on the premise that thoughts precede actions and that God-based thoughts bring about God-based actions. It shares anecdotes to help the reader understand their role in teaching children this most valuable lesson, and provides teaching modules to enable them to do so.

The reader is invited to slow down and change focus to look for a spiritual meaning and purpose to life then share what they have learned with a child. It speaks of the great potential of each child, and the child that lives within each of us, no matter what their circumstances, and how we, as adults, must nurture this potential so that it will blossom and flourish. The book is non-denominational.

MUSE IMAGERY™
9811 W. Charleston Blvd. Suite 2390, Las Vegas, NV 89117-7915
Phone 702-233-5910, Fax 702-233-1762, marketing@MUSEimagery.com

Muse Imagery Publishing
PRESENTS

Title: Connect	SETS Teaching Children How To With God
Author:	Shirley Hildreth
Retail Price:	$19.95
Distribution:	Ingram Book Group
Discount:	55%
ISBN No.:	0-9740500-0-8
LOC Control No.:	2003094617
Edition:	First Edition
Binding Type:	Perfect
No. Pages:	128; illustrated
Season:	Winter, 2003
Category (BISG Major subjects):	Religion (adult)/Family and Relationships/Self-Help
Intended Audience:	Parents, clergy and teachers of children in a religious setting, extended family members, psychologists, and caregivers of children.
Promotional Plans:	Author tour, space advertising, direct mail, writer's conferences
Trademarks:	SETS: Spiritually Enlightening Thoughts and Muse Imagery are trademarks of Muse Imagery LLC, a Nevada Limited Liability Company
Endorsements:	Mark Andrews, Emmy Award winning photographer
(back cover)	Roberta and Richard VandeVoort, Marriage and Family Therapists

Description:
SETS instructs the reader how to teach the most important lesson they will ever teach a child. This proven method builds on the premise that thoughts precede actions and that God-based thoughts bring about God-based actions. It invites the reader to slow down, change focus and look for a spiritual meaning and purpose to life, then share what they have learned with a child. Detailed teaching modules are provided to enable them to do so. Anecdotes are also included to emphasize the great potential of each child.

As this book demonstrates, SETS once learned, will play a vital role in the lives of children who will be expected, with honor and unflinching resolve, to play leading roles in the future of our communities. SETS is non-denominational.

Forthcoming Books By The Author:
SETS Musings Of The Spirit
SETS I Know You're There!
SETS A Glimpse Of Heaven

MUSE IMAGERY • 9811 W. Charleston Blvd. Suite 2390 • Las Vegas, NV 89117

Muse ImageryFacsimile Transmittal Sheet

To: Shauna L. Jones
From: Marketing Director
                MUSE IMAGERY
Fax Number: 702-123-4567
Phone Number: 702-123-4567
E-Mail: marketing@museimagery.com

Total number of pages 1

Re: BOOK REVIEW ACKNOWLEDGMENT

We have received the book review galley(s) for: SETS™ Teaching
Children How To Connect With God.

® We expect to review this book on
_____

® We expect to review this book, however the exact date is uncer-
tain at this time.

® Please send photograph of book.
     E-mail Address _____

® Please send photograph of author.
     E-mail Address _____

® We are sorry, we did not find your book suitable for review at
this time.

Additional Comments:
_____
_____
_____
_____

MUSE IMAGERY · 9811 W. Charleston Blvd. Suite 2390 · Las Vegas, NV 89117

Appendix B

Sample Query Letters

Sample Query Letter

STRANGER TO MYSELF
A NOVEL
BY Catherine L. de Lafontaine

Stranger to Myself addresses the cause and effect of co-dependency coupled with borderline personality disorder. Much like the characters portrayed in 'I Hate You – Don't Leave Me', Kitty, the protagonist, encompasses the self-defeating, self-fulfilling prophecies of a borderline personality. Throughout the novel, we see Kitty trying to work past co-dependency issues as depicted in 'The Co-dependents' Guide to the Twelve Steps'.

Stranger to Myself is told through the eyes of Kitty, a beautiful, sultry woman in her late twenties. Kitty is desperately trying to grasp control of her life as she experiences the mental anguish of yet another failed marriage, a second divorce. Barely able to carry on and without the benefit of a high school diploma, Kitty is determined to provide for her two children under the age of five. Kitty does not realize her life is unraveling quickly and that the solid ground beneath her feet is really a bog drowning her. Without seeing the impact of the path she is following, she becomes her own victim.

It is by giving away a part of herself, the vulnerable part, that Kitty momentarily satisfies the open wound within her. Impregnated with feelings of inadequacy, she ventures further into the flavorful world of the unexpected. Eventually the thin line becomes blurred between reality and what becomes acceptable. Kitty's instinct of survival kicks in and she brutally throws herself into a Pandora's Box of deceit and prostitution when she makes the decision to become and adult entertainer.

Alone, afraid, and without direction, now Kitty is caught in a web of self-loathing. She endures a world where mobsters loom and broken hearts collect, daily. She strips for money. She strips for attention. She strips for love and affection. In her psyche she wishes she could find the love that has evaded her. In her passionate lap dances, she is pleading; her body is screaming out just to be caressed the way a true love finds joy in pleasing his mate. The dismay awakens her when she realizes yet another time that she is simply pleasing another 'John' for money. The devastation slaps her hard when she realizes this man is just another nobody in her world.

A co-dependent lives within a dysfunctional relationship where toxic love prevails. According to the Borderline Personality Disorder Research Foundation, roughly 60 million people area affected by borderline personality disorder themselves or are touched by it through someone they know. *Stranger to Myself* creates awareness as to the daunting struggle of someone dealing with co-dependent behavior and borderline personality disorder, and because these disorders are widespread, the novel *Stranger to Myself* appeals to both sexes and all ages.

I would be pleased to submit all or part of my novel for your review. I may be reached at the following phone numbers and email address: Home (123) 456-7890, Cell (123) 456-7890, or Email anyauthor@hotmail.com. I look forward to hearing from you shortly and thank you for your consideration.

Sincerely,
Catherine L. de Lafontaine

(Catherine has several agents interested in reviewing her book.)

Sample Query Letter

Basketball and Past Lives
Written by award-winning filmmaker
Ken Feinberg

"Rudy" meets "What Dreams May Come" in this novel by award-winning filmmaker, published playwright and LA Drama Critics Circle Award nominated playwright Ken Feinberg. Screenplay and feature film to follow.

As a senior at the University of Alabama, Ace makes a surprise impression on basketball Coach Hill in a charity basketball game. In the game, Ace covers Alabama star and NCAA tournament MVP "Ice". When Coach Hill departs to coach in the NBA, he invites Ace to camp for a try out along with #1 draft pick Ice. Not only does Ace make the team, but he also becomes the catalyst that catapults he, Ice and the lowly Atlanta Hawks toward its first championship run.

During the Championship series, Coach Fitzsimmons, of the Timberwolves, will do anything to win a championship ring after being denied for so long. He sends his two ruffians in the game to explicitly knock Ace out of it. They knock Ace too hard, sending him out of the game and into a coma.

While Ace lay unconscious in the hospital, he experiences his last two lives: One as Simon, a Jewish museum curator in Berlin Germany, just before the war, and the other as Kahiga, an American Indian shaman in training. As the shaman, Kahiga time travels forward in time and witnesses his demise in Germany. Then, he visits Ace (himself) in the hospital coma.

Kahiga explains to Ace about the mistakes he keeps repeating each lifetime, and how his decision now will affect his past lives as well as his future lives. Ace has the decision to opt out now and start over, or make some major changes in his life.

Ace sees how Ice has been his best friend in many lives, Coach Hill, his mentor, and Coach Fitzsimmons and his two goons as recurring enemies.

Basketball and Past Lives is a great story that combines action/sports with metaphysical insight and drama. For young adult readers as well as adult readers.

Thank you for your consideration. I look forward to hearing from you.

Sincerely,

Ken Feinberg
123 Any Street
Your Town, USA

(Ken received almost two dozen positive replies to his query letter.)

Sample Query Letter

Carol Abrahamson
124 Your Street
Anytown, USA

Have you ever thought how convenient it would be to have an ironing board (maybe one that pulls down from the wall) and the electrical outlet for an iron built into your walk-in closet? Or drawers instead of toe kick baseboards in your kitchen for your serving platters and large, shallow pans? Or a deep sink near your garage entry for messy cleanups you'd rather not track through the house? Or electrical outlets inside bathroom drawers for both hiding and using your hair dryer, electric shaver, etc. while never unplugging them? *Best Ideas for the Built-in Features That Will Make Any Home Extraordinary* will be an encyclopedic collection of more than 500 similar ideas to consider when renovating, remodeling, or building a home.

What do they have in common? All are items to include in any size home and they each work with any décor or style home. They are not about materials, finishes, or "look," but add convenience and function. They are not about decoration or architecture, but are built-in features. They are not instructional how-tos, but are ideas. Most are inexpensive when designed into a project's initial plan, yet they all have the potential to make any home truly special! There is something fabulous in this book for every reader to want in his or her home!

Virtually all the current house and home books focus on decorating ideas, architectural elements, floor plans, or are how-to home improvement or repair books. While many of the ideas in *Best Ideas* can be found some-here, some-there in various shelter publications and TV programs and inside actual homes, no one has yet compiled a master idea book like this.

The 26 million home owners who complete renovations or remodels annually will love it, as will the million Americans who are actively planning to build a custom home next year or after. So will the 400,000 property owners who will build custom homes this year, and the million-plus architects and building contractors who advise these various owners.

I have spent three years researching these ideas for my own first custom home, wanting the ultimate in creature comfort at less than an ultimate cost. This book will save readers hundreds of hours of similar research and will expose them to possibilities they might never discover otherwise.

A successful consultant since 1983, I organize and sell ideas to my corporate clients (Apple, Yahoo! and 150 others) and generate, critique and edit their financial and public relations materials. I have also written a series of seven idea books (self-published) that assembled and organized the several hundred fragmented ideas that embodied the investor relations profession into one place for the first time.

I am currently consulting to enhance the residential plans of home and property owners, and I hope to start conducting *Best Ideas* seminars next year. My goal is to become nationally known for this area of expertise. My mission is to dramatically increase the number of built-in convenience features of all American homes at every price level.

Would you like to learn more about *Best Ideas*? I am eager to hear from you by phone, mail, or email at your convenience. Thank you.

Very truly yours,

Carol Abrahamson

(Carol received 64 requests from agents for her proposal package. Carol interviewed by telephone all who had an interest after seeing the proposal and narrowed her list to eight favorites. She went with one who had talked to McGrawHill about her book before she made her final choice.)

Sample Query Letter

Tammie Rothermel
P.O. Box 1234
Yourtown, USA

Nevermore?

Just as Scarlett seared her indelible brand on the South, Nikki in Nevermore? carves a swath across Continental Europe with her rock star husband, then conquers the rest of the universe with a music career of her own. Nikki flourishes inside fame's tornado; her marriage doesn't. Pursued by a seductively mysterious stranger, Nikki backs into the intrigue of the spy world only to discover the love of her life and a desperate situation that threatens to menace them for eternity.

Plucked from the pastoral hills of Pennsylvania, Nikki grows up fast at the hands of internationally renowned Merseyman Grant Henderson. To survive the rigors of life in the kaleidoscopic whirl of rock music, Nikki summons her grit and ingenuity. But a chance meeting with the "Agency," redefines her life. Honing her cunning to a razor's edge, Nikki triumphs over each obstacle, then dares the Agency to serve up more. Thriving on the edge she manages to steal the heart of Alexander.

The continental savior faire of playboy Alexander Vincente both entices and infuriates Nikki. His secret life jeopardizes their budding relationship, as he takes

Nikki on an impassioned romp through a society loftier than the new millionaires in her music milieu. As the love of her life and her eternal protector, his vow to love her "beyond life itself" consumes him.

With its seeds in the British music invasion, Nevermore? follows Nikki's rags-to-riches tale through her stormy liaison with Grant. Rising from the ashes of a failed marriage, Nikki then ignites her own white-hot rock career. But once she flashes her mesmerizing turquoise eyes in Alexander's direction it delivers the self-possessed Mr. Vincente to his knees.

Together and separately Nikki and Alexander roll the dice with their lives as they encounter double-dealing intrigue inside the clutches of the "Agency." From opulent Europe to gritty back alleys of Hong Kong they pursue life; right up until Alex, from the grave, delivers his beloved into the arms of another man. ... Or does he?

(Tammie's book was published in 2006 and is available worldwide.)

Sample Query Letter

Michelle DeAngelis
123 Any Street, Santa Monica, CA 90405
anyauthor@aol.com
123-345-6789 www.authorname.com

Dear [Literary Agent]:

In the tradition of groundbreaking books such as *Who Moved My Cheese?*, *Don't Sweat the Small Stuff*, and *You: The Owner's Manual*, *Get a Life That Doesn't Suck* compels the reader to get out of the rut he is in and make better choices. As the title suggests, *Get a Life That Doesn't Suck* is written to appeal to the reader who wants Deepak Chopra in a David Sedaris state of mind. It is wisdom served up as street-smart joy: an irreverent take on how to live life and love the ride. *Get a Life* is written by consultant, speaker, and coach, Michelle DeAngelis, who has been bringing a healthy dose of reality and life-affirming change to corporate America for nearly twenty years.

In *Get a Life That Doesn't Suck*, Michelle meets people in their misery and provides the antidote to common problems that make life seem like a succession of bad days: frustration, anger, hopelessness, feeling stuck, without energy, "checked out", paralyzed by indecision. Each of these obstacles to a joyful life is tackled with humor and real-life stories, as well as step-by-step instructions that guide the reader through the mechanics of choosing on purpose, and then owning the consequences of those choices.

Get a Life That Doesn't Suck appeals to the same audiences that loved books such as *The Joy Diet*, *How We Choose to Be Happy*, and the *Chicken Soup for the Soul* series, which prove the demand for practical and engaging books about personal power, inspiration, and human potential. The primary buyer for *Get a Life That Doesn't Suck* will be the self-improvement junkie who is continuously looking for the new and better way. The secondary buyer will be those who know people whose lives suck, and will also include career counselors, corporate human resource departments, and other professionals touting personal accountability.

Get a Life That Doesn't Suck makes it "okay" to be in a joyless existence—but not for long. It reminds us, in a playful and engaging way, how ill-equipped we are to deal with the challenges in life. Few of us are taught how to effectively work our way through problems and difficulties. Most people are taught to rail, complain, and feel victimized that things never go their way. *Get a Life That Doesn't Suck* reminds the reader what so many have forgotten or overlooked: we always have a choice. But choosing takes guts, and most people don't bother to summon the courage when it's easier to blame someone else.

The book consists of three basic sections:

• *You Are Here.* Where IS that exactly? This part includes tools to determine the reader's starting point, such as the Joy Quotient Quiz, which gives the reader his "JQ" and measures the internal gap between his beliefs and his actions. The reader is given a chance to pick himself out of a line-up of dismal circumstances, ranging from bored, lonely, and without purpose, to mad, hung over, and racked with guilt. If it sucks, *Get a Life That Doesn't Suck* can help.

• *The Aha!s.* These are the basic principles to live by—the keys to the *Get a Life* kingdom—explained through irresistible stories about real people learning lessons and having fun, and they are pivotal in getting the audience from where they are now, to where they want to be. These are not vague clichés, nor platitudes. The Aha!s outline the specific steps to choosing the life you want in everyday moments of truth.

• *The Other Side.* You might even miss complaining. Once you are able to embody the Aha!s and narrow your joy gaps, here's what's on the other side: waking up happy and refreshed, having enough energy throughout the day, being able to say 'no' when you need to, losing those 15 pounds, getting that promotion, even dealing with the jackass at the dry cleaners. You chose. Next thing you know, you have a Life.

For those who are sick and tired of being sick and tired, *Get a Life That Doesn't Suck* offers a better way to go through every day. *Get a Life* encourages the reader to learn what makes him happy, what reduces his worry, what improves his outlook, what he needs to let go of, and how to do that. It makes joy accessible, and it makes the concept of enjoying life a tangible one, not an airy-fairy dream.

The journey from blame to personal power and account-ability is not an easy one, but *Get a Life* makes it worth the trip.

Sincerely,

Michelle DeAngelis

(Michelle received thirty-four positive replies to her query letter.)

Sample Query Letter

PIGEONS UNDER THE RADAR

As in the tradition of authors such as John Grishman where ordinary persons are given the opportunity to do extraordinary things, so in my book Rosco Rawlings, retired police sergeant, is afforded such when he accidentally notices the crate in which he shipped baby racing pigeons to Europe was tampered with. The reader is introduced to the world of pigeon racing where enthusiasts from blue collar to royalty obsess over races, prize money, and pedigrees their world wide sport offers.

Fierce comradeships exist among members of hundreds of racing clubs around the world. Members of Rosco's local club become enraged at the thought their sport is being used for criminal purposes and vow to get to the bottom of the mystery even though authorities tell them they are grasping at straws. Rosco's son a professor at the local medical school is able to bring cutting edge technology to bear and convinces HOMELAND SECURITY to investigate the matter. A clever under the radar method of transporting data to terrorist cells is uncovered and eliminated. Another tentacle of terrorism is sheared in the ongoing war by the spirit of ordinary men who rise to the occasion when the curiosity of one man points the way.

I will be happy to provide any material you may request.
Sincerely,

Dr. Fran Hagaman
Clinical Professor of Psychiatry
123 Any Road
Yourtown, USA

(Fran received 10 positive replies within the first 24 hours.)

Sample Query Letter

The Heart's Way:
For The Recovering Intellectual

Have we become a society of walking heads? Many of us have hidden our true selves and heart's destiny behind a wall of intellectual accomplishments, advanced degrees, self-aggrandizing job titles or perfectionist personas. The busyness of our lives often prevents us from noticing our heart's voice is screaming out for attention. How many of us work 17 hour days six or seven days a week and have little time to spend with our families? Cell phones, e-mail, black-berry's, pocket PC's all make us globally available around the clock. We wonder why we have over a 50% divorce rate, illness due to job stress and children fighting for their parent's attention. Now is the time for this book because we are a society that has lost touch with our hearts.

What Julia Cameron's, "The Artist's Way" did for awakening the artist within, "The Heart's Way for the Recovering Intellectual" does for the majority of us who have hidden the voice of our heart behind our intellectual accomplishments.

The audience for this book is vast, as it will speak to anyone who wants a greater connection with their hearts. The book is also for those of us who may remotely identify with being a recovering intellectual. Recovering intellectuals are often found in corporate executive and professional offices, academic institutions, or hiding their true selves behind a myriad of other facades.

Business, corporate, educational, spiritual, and nonprofit organizations as well as ministers, therapists, counselors, doctors, and anyone who loves a recovering intellectual will help promote and popularize this book.

Dr. Lamm walks among the recovering intellectuals with her doctorate from Columbia University, an endless list of other assorted achievements and certifications, and 18 years of global coaching, consulting and academic experience working with recovering intellectuals. Oprah magazine quoted Dr. Lamm as an expert in personal transformation. She beautifully weaves this expertise into the core foundation of this book.

The book begins with a fun quiz to determine just how much of a recovering intellectual you really are. It is then designed around a 13-week program to recover your heart including real life short stories, transformative exercises, meditations and specific weekly heart dates that will capture the buried heart of any recovering intellectual. Chapter 1 describes how to use the book which can be done individually or as part of a support group. The next 13 chapters are arranged around an acronym that spells "Open Your Heart." Week one is "O" for Opening to Receive; Week two is "P" for Purpose; "E" is for Expression, and "N" for Nurturing, etc. The book concludes with how to integrate your newfound heart connection into your life.

For the "off the charts" recovering intellectual, this book can be done multiple times uncovering new layers of the heart each time. This book is guaranteed to make a difference in the hearts of everyone who reads it. To receive a copy of a proposal along with some sample material or to discuss this project more fully with Sharon, please feel free to contact her at youremail@hotmail.com or 123-456-7890

Dr. Sharon Lamm

(Sharon sent out two different query letters in a four-month period and received over seventy positive replies.)

Sample Query Letter

Shelly Marie Gaul
123 Your Street
Anytown, USA
University Of Arizona Degree, 1993
Degree Major: Creative Writing
E-mail: authorname@aol.com

Reverse!

"Reverse" is a novel that examines the distorted relationship between what a person wants to see and what is truly real. As people present themselves to the world, how many choose to make themselves appear exactly the way they would like others to see them, hiding the depths of their depravity from the public eye, when our very lives might depend on seeing the truth?

Melinda Franklin, the mother of psychic, nine-year-old twins, is a woman abused and on the run. For years she has blocked out her natural instincts, choosing to see people for their surface value, in turn denying her heritage even while her children begin to exhibit some of the same signs of reading minds and seeing into the future. After they flee to Tucson, Melinda meets Dave Nuback, a singer in a bar that draws her to him with his haunting melodies. Despite her fear of all men, Melinda begins to trust this mysterious stranger enough to lower the invisible walls she has erected around herself.

Elementary school teacher, Michael Romas, has his own share of demons in the closet. Disfigured at birth, he has had to deal with bullying all his life. Now as an adult he must live with the guilt of the death of his tormentors and learn to allow someone close enough to see the person he really is underneath. When he meets the Franklins, his hermit-like world begins to crumble, despite Melinda's own abrasiveness and pity. In sharp contrast, Dave Nuback struggles every day with the desire to find the right woman, the one who will erase all of the unfinished business in his life. When he first meets Melinda, he is struck by how perfect she fits the part.

One of these men has a dark side, bent on revenge and wanting to recreate a grizzly past. He cannot rest until he rewrites history, turning the tables on those who tortured him. Will Melinda listen to her children and decipher their hidden messages before it is too late? Which man will Melinda choose in the end when one man threatens her very existence and the lives of two other women? Will she be able to embrace her own psychic abilities anew and look at what lies beneath the surface? It may be too late because the curtain has raised and the play already begun.

For further questions and/or information, I may be reached at (123) 456-7890 or by E-mail at youremail@aol.com. I look forward to hearing from you.

Sincerely,

Shelly Marie Gaul

(Shelly received several positive replies to her query letter.)

Query Letter Sample

In the tradition of YOUR ERRONEOUS ZONES, which gave people a glimpse as to how their thinking affects their relationships on earth, THE GOD ZONE gives a glimpse as to how our thinking affects the evolution of our soul. We are spiritual beings having a physical experience and our purpose in life is to realize our divine nature.

My book, THE GOD ZONE, gives an eye opening, easy to understand overview of how science and spirituality were erroneously separated during the time of Roman Empire. I explain how these two systems of beliefs must be integrated once again in the minds of human beings for the evolution of our souls.

From Edgar Cayce to astrology to quantum physics, there is truth to be found in many sources. THE GOD ZONE takes all this information into account, making it truly a handbook for higher consciousness.

Using principles from quantum physics and spirituality, including the Bible, THE GOD ZONE shows how the human race is on the verge of realizing their divine nature. The tools for tapping into the power within to direct our destiny through our thinking is revealed in an entertaining, easy to read style.

THE GOD ZONE will appeal to the masses, including my 78 million fellow baby boomers. Many are frustrated that their lives, once committed to making the world a more peaceful place, have been too busy building families and careers to follow their dreams of the sixties. The information in my book can help rekindle the dreams left behind and give new hope and a new way of looking at life.

Those who find comfort in books written by Deepak Chopra, Marianne Williamson, Wayne Dyer and Joel Osteen will like my book. Dalai Lama's new book, THE UNIVERSE IN A SINGLE ATOM gives a glimpse of the truth that is now bubbling to the surface.

In THE GOD ZONE,

- you quiet our internal dialogue

- you tune into your higher power, leading to your highest good

- your perception of reality changes, thus changing your reality

- you become part of the solution

THE GOD ZONE teaches powerful techniques for transmuting stress and fear into an energy that will help heal the world.

My website, THEGODZONE.COM is currently under construction.

Dr. Fran Addeo

(Dr. Addeo received over twenty-five positive replies to her query letter.)

Sample Query Letter

Building Serenity

Dear [Literary Agent]

In the tradition of the Kevin Kline film, *Life as a House*, *Building Serenity* establishes the construction of one's own home as the culmination of a life's work. With over 2 million new homes as well as countless renovations completed each year, each one unique with a unique set of players, we approach what should be an exciting event with an undue combination of apprehension and dread.

We have all heard the horror stories, are loathe to give strangers the run of our homes, see our homes as an extension of ourselves and cherish our privacy. Yet we lack the skills and/or time to perform the work ourselves. Thus, with much trepidation, we turn over our largest asset to strangers, whom we do not often trust, to perform work that we really do not understand.

It's no wonder that homeowners are afraid from the start. That fear leads to natural defensiveness and overprotective reactions. Mixed into this witches' brew are the very different players, each with unique backgrounds, motivations as well as fears. Those backgrounds of the individuals involved in a new home are as varied as those of the general population, yet, uniquely they must all work towards a single goal. Communication between the diverse group becomes essential, but it often very poorly handled.

Unlike the plethora of "How-to" books on the market, *Building Serenity* provides the millions of homeowners with a basic set of tools to understanding the whole process in a clear, concise and light-hearted manner that all readers, regardless of their building experience level will enjoy.

Building Serenity delves into the issues:

· Why we build homes the way we do. A brief historical perspective on the American Dream of single-family homes.

· How it should be done correctly. The most important basics that so often lead to poorly built homes. The reader learns what to look for and how to make sure it is done right. The basic tools (legal and insurance) homeowners should use to protect themselves.

· Who homeowners will be working with and what that person's problems and motivations are. This section includes contractors, subcontractors, engineers, architects and building inspectors.

Thus, armed with some knowledge and empathy, and basic legal protections the homeowner can approach the whole process with less fear. Building and renovating our homes can become a time of renewal to ultimately improve the way we live by providing the nurturing home environment that we seek as well as contributing to our understanding of others.

Respectfully,

James P. Mills, Jr.
123 Your Street
Anytown, USA
(123) 123-4567 voice, (123) 123-1234 fax
authorname@yahoo.com
www.buildingserenity.com

(Jimmy received thirty-five positive replies to his query letter.)

Sample Query Letter

MEET YOUR DREAM MATE IN TWELVE MONTHS.... OR LESS

A relationship that works is as good as it gets. When relationships don't work, they make being single look like a trip to the beach. The working relationship has soul, sense, and sex all of which require both emotional intelligence and maturity.

The current books on the subject explain the process of meeting and mating, but don't attempt the depth of self-analysis that goes into a truly emotionally intelligent match or the attitude adjustment that makes a courtship fun and a marriage/relationship viable.

The target audience is women in their 20's to 50's. The fluidity of our marriage bonds means a broader base of prospective readers—those in the market and those returning for the 1st or 2nd time. Other prospective purchasers are all the people weary of hearing the complaints.

In my class at Emory University in Atlanta, "I Will Be Married In A Year", unfailingly for 18 years, I've had about 20% on scholarships provided by their mothers, fathers, sons, daughters, or consortium of friends who were happy to underwrite the participant to put some muscle behind their mouth and acquire some new topics of conversation.

Covered topics are: To find a soul mate, you need a soul; The only place you won't meet someone is home alone; Yes, you do have to be loved for yourself, but they still have to want to meet you; Use business skills to get a mate; You wouldn't take a job based on the office building; No one wants to be married to get ignored; De-blame yourself and others: character assassination is terrible fore-play; Never cheat or lie to anyone with a memory; and Don't marry without knowing the emotional price and wanting to pay it.

Lessons to be learned are what to change and how, where to go, planning a spouse shopping list, resources to cull, strengthening intimacy capability, and how to spot a keeper.

The action format of the twelve-month plan is essential to accomplishing the goal. A year is too soon to marry but deadlines and goal-setting work; and if the class were titled " How to marry in five years", no one would start until the fourth year.

The track record from the course, based on an Emory survey two years later, showed one out of four participants married or engaged. Nels, a student from 18 years ago, got married within the year. He describes the course as the best money he's ever spent and his marriage as the perfect fairy tale happy ending.

Dr. Janet Page

(Dr. Page received over 30 positive replies from literary agents to her query letter. Her agent is presently shopping her book to publishers.)

Sample Query Letter

MAUREEN SIOBHAN MOORE, ESQ.
123 Any Street, EL PRADO, NM 87529   (123) 123-1234
anyauthor@aol.com

The Mistresses Club

The Mistresses Club combines strong, funny, outspoken, believable characters like those in Jennifer Crusie's Welcome to Temptation, with a underlying message of hope like Marian Keyes's Rachel's Holiday and Lucy Sullivan is Getting Married. But there are also shades of Armistead Maupin's Tales of the City in this novel about nine people—eight women and one gay man—all of whom are involved with married men in small-town Jamaica, Indiana.

Bright, witty, red-headed realtor Sally Van Neal, dumpy, straight-laced church secretary Marci Ferguson, and glamorous yet vulnerable African-American artist Desiree Thomas are the three main characters. When Sally starts a support group for mistresses, based loosely on the principles of AA, she meets Marci, who is in love with a member of her church choir, and Desiree, whose lover delights in keeping her on an emotional rollercoaster.

They are joined by paralegal JoAnn Renart, whose steel-trap mind is concealed by shaggy hair and Coke-bottle glasses; twenty-two year old Tiffani Calder, who appears to be a stereotypical dumb blonde, and Elise Jensen, a forty-something English teacher. Gay interior designer Jesse Squires and Gina Smithson Delacourt, the richest woman in town, round out the original group. Later, after much denial, hairdresser Lisa Shepherd joins them. Their lives interweave in chance encounters at Sunday brunches, hair appointments and a bar mitzvah, as well as in their weekly meetings.

As The Mistresses come to know each other better, deep, supportive friendships develop, sometimes between the most unlikely partners. Jesse and almost-homophobic Marci become close when she helps him in his relationship with Gina's husband. Sally, who hated Elise in high school, is a rock of support when Elise's lover kills himself. Tiffani turns to Marci, who is shocked to the core at Tiffani's family history of murder and prostitution, but is able to help her see that she is not condemned to repeat the past. When Desiree's boyfriend breaks up with her publicly, Elise is there to pick up the pieces, and Desiree eventually finds enough strength to reject him and go to Greece to paint. With help from Lisa, JoAnn gets the courage to apply to law school and leave Jamaica—and then her lover's wife tells him she wants a divorce. Marci's lover breaks up with her, and she finds a new job, a deeper faith, and a new love interest. Gina master-minds a plot to save Roger and Jesse's relationship even as she questions her motives in continuing to see her own lover. After much soul-searching and help from Lisa, Sally stays with her boyfriend, with a bittersweet knowing that their relationship is doomed. As the novel ends, some of the characters are in love relationships, some are alone, but all have grown and changed as a result of being members of The Mistresses Club.

Their desires and motivations are as old as the Bible and as current as Desperate Housewives.

(Maureen received many positive replies to her query and is presently being represented by agent Ken Atchity.)

Sample Query Letter

Jeanne Guthrie
123 Your Street
Anytown, USA
123-123-1234

Dear [Literary Agent];

MYSTIC RED

The novel MYSTIC RED takes an unprecedented, bold step forward to explain the relationship between spirit guides and people they assist. From the Oracle at Delphi to Joan of Arc to Edgar Cayce, cultures have been fascinated by those who receive messages from the Divine. MYSTIC RED brings into reality the daily communications that any of us—baby, teenager, or adult—have with our spirit guides.

Fourteen-year-old Red Donovan adores basketball, despises her freckles, and reads romance novels to understand love. She blames herself when her parents divorce. Then she rebels as her father Philip moves them 350 miles from her mom and friends.

Philip Donovan is the Donald Trump of Philadelphia. After he pushes away his wife Dorothy, he turns to Red for love and support. But Red is angry at him over the divorce and relocation to Pittsburgh.

Spirit guide Paul appears to Red as an 11-year-old Dutch boy dressed in white clothes. During games of one-on-one or just hanging out, he teaches Red about unconditional love. Paul also watches interactions between Red and her family from his viewing room on the Fifth Dimension.

Dorothy Donovan leaves her passion behind to be an obedient and submissive wife. After the divorce, she gets her act together and follows her dream of teaching.

Red opens to and accepts Paul with the innocence of a newborn. This allows him to teach her to become a lightening bolt and change the weather. She also exists on different dimensions, experiences déjà vu in Sphere Time, and forgives those who hurt her most. Red experiences travels to a Golden Dimension and the Center of the Universe. Through these lessons, Red finally understands and accepts unconditional love. With Paul, she's happier than ever.

Philip, on the other hand, rejects Paul. Philip believes the worst—that Paul intends to kill his daughter. So Philip forbids Red from speaking to Paul again.

Now Red faces the choice to obey her father or her heart. Philip must decide whether to listen to Paul's persistent messages or continue to live in anguish.

When Red and Philip connect with Paul, they make the highest choices that lead them to peace and unconditional love. Then they naturally accept and support each other. No more control. No more rebellion. Philip evens takes the initiative to reconcile with Dorothy. At last, they receive the healing they've sought for years.

Messages come to people everyday from their spirit guides. Often, they are unheard or ignored. When people understand the loving intent of spirit guides, they open to possibilities beyond their wildest imagination. Their childhood wounds are healed, and they live without fear.

Sincerely,

Jeanne Guthrie

(Jeanne's agent is presently shopping her book to publishers.)

Sample Query Letter

Enclosed is a query for the book, Forgiveness: The Ultimate Freedom. As you can see by the enclosed letter, I have already received an endorsement from the Dalai Lama for this book.

Dr. Eileen R. Borris-Dunchunstang
Dir. of Training - The Institute for Multi-Track Diplomacy
123 Your Street
Anytown, USA

Forgiveness: The Ultimate Freedom

In a world fraught with hatred and violence all of us will be placed in situations challenged by issues of forgiveness. Just as Neale Donald Walsh in his books on "Conversations with God" has helped us realize that spirituality is at our finger tips, "Forgiveness: The Ultimate Freedom" will show us how we can transform our consciousness through the power of love and compassion.

The essence of this book opens people's hearts to forgive offering the all illusive "peace of mind" we all seek. The audience for this work is unlimited, ranging from the abused to the abuser, from the young to the old, covering both genders and including millions of care givers.

Through stories beginning with your next door neighbor to interviews with one of our greatest spiritual leaders and with people from all walks of life who have experienced personal struggles and tragedies from the personal to the political, readers will gain a deeper understanding of the psychological and spiritual landscape of forgiveness from its difficulties to its greatest rewards. With each story are chapters which talk about the different concepts of forgiveness as they relate to each story. The book ends with how forgiveness can be used not only at the individual level but in the political arena as well.

In the process of learning how to forgive we begin to question all the values and beliefs we hold. Haven't we had enough pain? Perhaps it is through our struggles with our pain that we recognize we can make different choices. It is through these choices that we can change our thinking and change our consciousness which can ultimately change the world.

Thank-you for your consideration. I look forward to hearing from you.

Sincerely,

Dr. Eileen R. Borris
President - the American Psychological Association
Division 48 – Peace Psychology
123-123-1234
authoremail@hotmail.com

(Eileen's book is being published by McGraw-Hill under the title, *Finding Forgiveness: A Seven Step Program for Letting go of Anger and Bitterness*. There are a number of countries that bought the first version of the book . When her agent got the book, five countries at the London Book fair bought it right away. They were Germany, Brazil, Japan, Portugal and Poland. The US only wanted a self-help version so Eileen wrote a second book proposal and McGraw-Hill literally snatched it up. According to her agent there are a number of countries interested in the book and are waiting for it to come out in the US.)

Query Letter Sample

Ellen Rosson
1234 Your Street
Anytown, USA
123-123-1234
authoremail@comcast.net

Attached is a query letter for my novel, *Expiration Date*, which is a fictional tale of one family and yet reflects the story of so many. Although fictional, this work is loosely based on my personal experiences. Born to parents as they turned forty, by my early twenties we were facing the loss of one parent and the illness of the other. This story of family secrets that should have been shared is set in my small Southern hometown. *Expiration Date* floats along the Tennessee River unwinding along the way a relevant story for so many readers who find themselves similarly situated, or are working to avoid it.

I thank you for your time and look forward to hearing from you.

Sincerely,
Ellen Rosson

EXPIRATION DATE

The man who never cared for his youngest daughter falls ill at a time in Rachel's life when everything else is right where she wanted. Newly married and recently relocated to accept the job opportunity for which she crafted her career, Rachel finds herself back in the waiting room of her home-town hospital. Convinced that once again her father is doing anything he can to spoil her plans, the best Rachel can do is devise a plan to care for him while walking the fine line between balancing her own life and being toppled again by the rejection of a man who admittedly does not want her help.

Expiration Date unravels a lifetime of half-truths, as the story flows along the river where the Townsend family has lived for generations. From hospital waiting room, to front porch swing, through assisted living and into nursing homes wonderfully rich and original characters visit on a journey from Alabama into Tennessee. The stories that had been held back for years flood Rachel's mind and wash over her memories to erase the scrapbook images of Homer Townsend. The tales told by these visitors are about a man that Rachel never knew. The man turns out to be her father. The torrent of information erodes more than one lifetime of misunderstanding that served as a dam for decades, built by a grieving grandfather to keep the secrets of a different daughter.

Expiration Date speaks to the issues so many families face. As our population ages, many seniors fear the loss of their independence. Together with their children they will face end of life choices in not too distant days. This novel facilitates a discussion of long-term care, powers-of-attorney and family finances, subjects often postponed for less caustic conversations. Wrapped in the reality of one family's situation *Expiration Date* is a story of seeing clearly for the first time. Rachel is forced to examine who she really is, as well as what she truly wants. The fabric of her life begins to take on a pattern and texture different from the one she had covered herself with for over thirty years.

In the way Melinda Haynes' first novel Mother of Pearl told a profoundly moving story of life, love and the definition of family in the 1950's South, *Expiration Date* tells today's tale of choices, conflict and consensus in a family unwilling to talk about the truth when not knowing seems to be the only thing holding them together.

(Ellen received over a dozen positive replies to her query letter.)

Query Letter Sample

NANCY FISCHER
123 Your Street
Anytown, USA
123-123-1234

Dear [Literary Agent]:

CHOICES:
ESCAPING THE ILLUSION OF BEING A VICTIM

As evidenced by the success of Carolyn Myss' book, "Sacred Contracts," the world has accepted that before birth, we enter into agreements which determine what our life experiences will be. It is clear from Myss' work that every relationship is a sacred contract, even when it deals with sexual abuse.

Like no other book on this topic ever written before, "Choices: Escaping the Illusion of Being a Victim" takes the concept to a new level by showing us how we have the power to escape the illusion of victimhood because we actually created it.

This book is for anyone who has or knows of someone who has been abused and who are ready to break the pattern of being victims. It is also for those who work to help these "victims."

After nearly a half century of choosing to be a victim, sudden flashbacks of childhood incest propelled me into an extraordinary journey of self-discovery aided by many alternative therapies. With the realization that we create our own realities through the decisions we make, I escaped the illusion of being a victim and chose instead a life of empowerment and self love.

"Choices: Escaping the Illusion of Being a Victim" will free millions from the binding relationship of victim that we have created.

Sincerely,

Nancy Fischer

(Nancy's book is presently available at all major book stores, including Amazon.com.)

Sample Query Letter

50 Bible Facts You Need to Know
Before You Get to Heaven

Marion H. Williams
123 Your Street
Anytown, USA

Dear [Literary Agent],

The best-selling success of Mitch Albom's the five people that you meet in heaven demonstrates that the general public continues to be curious about the afterlife. My book imagines that the afterlife begins with a biblical challenge from St. Peter. He initially welcomes you and acknowledges your strong belief, good works, and generosity. However, in order to pass through the gates of heaven, he requires you to name the four Gospels, locate the Lord's Prayer in the Bible, and quote three scripture passages. Does a blank look come across your face and does sweat start beading up on your forehead?

After attending and teaching numerous Sunday School classes, I became aware that I was not the only one who did not know the Fruits of the Spirit or the names of the twelve disciples off the top of my head. Many of us have a strong faith but lack a working knowledge of the Bible.

The purpose of this book is to give an overview of some important building blocks that most Christians should know but often do not. Furthermore, it is especially important for our children, and especially our teenagers, to know by heart some scripture passages that they can rely on when confronted with peer pressure. By equipping them with this knowledge, they will be better prepared to say "no" and walk away.

The audience for this book would be primarily non-fundamentalist Christians. Adults, children, and youth would enjoy reading it. This would be a small, pocket-size paperback book that would easily fit in a purse, jacket, or on a bed stand for easy reference. Distribution would be through both Christian and mainstream bookstores.

My manuscript is almost complete. If you would like to see my book proposal, or if you have any questions, please call me at 123-123-1234 or email me at authoremail@hotmail.com.

Thank you for your time and consideration.

Sincerely,

Marion H. Williams

(Marion's agent is presently shopping her book to publishers.)

Sample Query Letter

Good Work!
Choosing Joy on the Job

Through a deeper understanding of seeing, influencing, and creating joy at work, readers in any box on the organizational chart can take their next step towards freedom and joy by exercising their personal power on Monday. Like Tom Peters' In Search of Excellence, this book changes the way we see work, and so speaks not just to millions of business managers and leaders, but to workers, parents, teachers, coaches, and all those striving to make their work and the work of those around them joyful, meaningful, and effective.

The first section of the book unravels our misguided notions about joy, choice, and work, and replaces them with a workable vision. In the second section, readers learn to see joy in work, influence and spread joy in the workplace, and create joyful work situations, as they join the author in reconnecting with joy in childhood chores and activities, grunt work, boring office work, writing, campus politics, management, teaching, design, volunteering, and consulting. The final section provides practical principles of choosing joy, blocks that may prevent our joy, and actions to help readers move forward.

A life-long passion for empowering people, and years of experience improving business results as a change agent and coach led the author to develop and test practical steps and tools that help workers choose joy. Now he brings this passion to readers as he draws them to a new vision and practice at work.

Where's the joy in your work today?

Roger Wyer
123 Your Street
Anytown, USA

(Roger's book, which was released in 2006, is presently available at all major book stores, including Amazon.com.)

Appendix C
Example Literary Agent Replies

Sample Agent Reply

To: Dr. Sharon Lamm
From: DeFiore and Company

Thank you for your query letter and for your interest in our agency. I'm sorry to say that this project is not quite right for the specific talents of the people at our agency at this time.

We sincerely thank you again for thinking of us, however, and wish you the best of luck in finding the right path to publication.

Sincerely,

DeFiore and Company

Sample Agent Reply

To: Dr. Sharon Lamm
From: DeFiore and Company

Please send the full proposal for review.

Teresa Hartnett
The Hartnett Agency

Sample Agent Reply

To: Dr. Sharon Lamm
From: The Ned Leavitt Agency

Dear Dr. Lamm,
We have received your query letter regarding your two book projects and are interested in seeing more material. Please send a proposal for THE HEART'S WAY, and the first 50 pages of RE-BIRTH THROUGH BIRTH, along with a SASE to the following address:

The Ned Leavitt Agency
70 Wooster Street
New York, NY 10012

Make sure to include in the cover letter that this is requested material.
Please have patience in hearing back from us. It can take several weeks for us to process material. I assure you that you will hear from us when we have reached a decision on your submission.
Thanks for submitting!

Best,

The Ned Leavitt Agency

Sample Agent Reply

To: Dr. Sharon Lamm
From: Sebastian Agency

Dear Dr. Lamm,

While I am not a recovering intellectual, I would very much like to see your proposal package. It makes a lot of sense in theory and could be a wonderful book.

If you have not already committed yourself elsewhere, please send it hardcopy to my attention:

Laurie Harper
Sebastian Agency

Sample Agent Reply

To: Dr. Sharon Lamm
From: Castiglia Literary Agency

Dear Dr. Lamm,

Did you get an agent? I sent this on May 10, and didn't hear back...
Please confirm receipt.

*****

Dr. Lamm:
I'm an agent with the Castiglia Agency, and Julie Castiglia passed your query to me.
I would very much like to see your proposal. Please send to PO Box 8037, La Jolla, CA 92038.
Sounds fascinating.
Thanks.

Winifred Golden
Castiglia Literary Agency

Sample Agent Reply

To: Dr. Sharon Lamm
From: Sarah Jane Freymann

Dear Dr. Lamm,

I would love to see a proposal and smple chapters.

Sarah Jane Freymann

Sample Agent Reply

To: Dr. Sharon Lamm
From: Natasha Kern Literary Agency

Hi Sharon,

Please do send a copy of your proposal to me (see contact info at bottom). This is exactly right for my list (see that on my website at www.natashakern.com)

Warmly,

Natasha

Sample Agent Reply

To: Dr. Sharon Lamm
From: Wilson Devereux Company

Dear Dr. Lamm,

BD Barker has given me your submission for review. Ar e you available for a phone conversation with us Friday May 12th 2:30 pm est? Please reply with the appropriate telephone number.

Thank You,

Tony Frothingham
VP Acquisitions
Wilson Devereux Company

Sample Agent Reply

To: Anne
From: Harvey Klinger Agency

Thank you for your query. Your project does not sound right for us, but best of luck finding an enthusiastic agent and editor for your work.

In the future, please send your query to queries@harveyklinger.com

For a good idea of the types of projects we represent, we invite you to view our agency website: www.harveyklinger.com

Sample Agent Reply

To: Thomas Puetz
From: Shepard Agency

Thank you for thinking of us. However, we are not currently taking on new clients. Have you tried Writers' House at 21 West 26th Street, New York, N.Y.10010; 212-685-2400. Good luck.

The Shepard Agency

Sample Agent Reply

To: Paul Hall
From: Mildred Marmur Associates Ltd.

Dear Mr Hall,

Ms Lebowitz has decided to leave literary agenting.

Alas, this is a very small agency and the new work of current clients is keeping us over-busy and not able to consider material by new clients.

Your credentials are very impressive and we wish you the best of luck in finding representation, and a publisher, very soon.

Mildred Marmur Associates Ltd.

Sample Agent Reply

To: Shirley Hildreth
From: Creative Artists Agency

Dear Ms. Hildreth:

We received your e-mail inquiring about having Creative Artists Agency represent you for the above-entitled project. Although we appreciate your interest, we do not handle publishing at this time, moreover, we have a firm policy of returning all unsolicited material unread. Accordingly, we are forwarding your e-mail back to you and we have deleted your e-mail from our system.

Your unsolicited submission has not been, and will not be disclosed to any executive or other employee of Creative Artists Agency or any other person. You should be aware that many ideas are generated by our employees and our clients or other sources. To the extent that any projects are generated which contain elements similar to what you submitted, the similarities are purely coincidental.

Thank you for considering Creative Artists Agency. We wish you much luck in your endeavors.

Cordially,

CREATIVE ARTISTS AGENCY

Appendix D

Sample Book Proposals

A Sample Non-Fiction Proposal Package

A Proposal for

The Heart's Way

Being Good Enough
The Key to Unlocking Inner Peace

OR

The Heart's Way

Do you or someone you know need to
get back to who you really are or
discover yourself for the first time?

By Dr. Sharon Lamm-Hartman

Dr. Sharon Lamm-Hartman
PO Box 1234
Yourtown, USA
123-456-7890
author@msn.com
www.insideoutlearninginc.com

Table of Contents

Introduction

What Julia Cameron's, "The Artist's Way" did for struggling artists, "The Heart's Way" does for the recovering intellectual - those of us who have hidden the voice of our heart behind our invented personas, walls of achievements and busy life styles.

We have become a society of walking heads. We have hidden our true selves and heart's destiny behind a wall of accomplishments, advanced degrees, self-aggrandizing job titles or perfectionist personas. The busyness of our lives prevents us from noticing our heart's voice is screaming out for attention. How many of us work 17 hour days six or seven days a week and have little time to spend with our families? Cell phones, e-mail, blackberry's, pocket PC's all make us globally available around the clock. We wonder why we have over a 50% divorce rate, illness due to job stress and children fighting for their parent's attention. Now is the time for this book because we are a society that has lost touch with our hearts.

There are many books about opening one's heart, but most are associated with a religious orientation and none provide a simple step by step approach and transformative program based on years of award-winning research and experience. The Heart's Way is the first book to use a simple and profound 12-week transformative program to recover the hearts of the millions of people who will read and use this book. Thus the audience for this book is vast, as it will speak to anyone who wants a greater connection with their hearts. The book is also for those of us who may remotely identify with being a "recovering intellectual."

Dr. Sharon Lamm walks among the recovering intellectuals with her doctorate from Columbia University, an endless list of other assorted achievements and certifications, and 18 years of global coaching, consulting, speaking and academic experience working with recovering intellectuals like herself. Her research on personal transformation (upon which this book is based) received awards from the

Center for Creative Leadership and The Academy of Human Resource Development. Oprah magazine quoted Dr. Lamm as an expert in personal transformation. She beautifully weaves this expertise into the core foundation of this book.

A recovering intellectual has one or more of the following characteristics: 1) hides behind academic or professional titles and accomplishments or invented personas, 2) lives such a busy life style they have no time to hear their heart's voice, 3) needs to know too much and express too little, or 4) prefers to analyze and read about life instead of actually experiencing it. Recovering intellectuals are often found in corporate executive and professional offices, academic institutions or hiding their true selves behind a myriad of other facades.

Business, corporate, educational, spiritual, and nonprofit organizations as well as ministers, therapists, counselors, doctors, and anyone who loves a recovering intellectual will help promote and popularize this book.

A great addition to the book is that Dr. Lamm is bringing several "recovering intellectuals," including herself, along the journey as she completes the book. This group will participate in the weekly exercises and e-mail their results and reflections to Dr. Lamm who will include some of their real-life experiences in the book. Dr. Lamm also has hundreds of client stories who over the years have participated in the exercises in the book. She can draw on any number of these stories to help the reader feel they are not alone as they complete the "Heart's Way" program.

The book immediately grabs the reader's attention with a quiz that enables them to determine just how much of a recovering intellectual they really are. Chapter 1 describes a bit about the research and experience upon which the book is based and shares how to use the book which can be done individually or as part of a support group. The next 12 chapters are the transformative program that will recover readers' hearts. The book structure is arranged around an acronym "Open Your Heart." Week one is "O" for Opening to Receive;

Week two is "P" for Purpose; "E" is for Empathy, and "N" for Nurturing, etc. The book concludes with a bonus week "T" for Truth that provides the key to fully commit and decide to live a "Heart's Way" life.

The weekly programs are jam packed full of real life short stories, transformative exercises, meditations and specific weekly heart dates that will capture the buried heart of any recovering intellectual. Each week has unique and simple exercises to obtain the lessons for the week's topic. For example, week two "P" for Purpose includes an exercise to help readers connect with their unique purpose. This exercise is simple and is already selling on its own as a CD workbook called "Discover Your Life Purpose." The exercises come from years of research and experience on what facilitates personal transformation.

The book will include a folded insert of a poster-sized heart made up of 12 individual heart shapes. At the end of each week, the reader will summarize their key learning and take-aways from that week on a weekly summary page inside a dotted-line heart. Each week the reader will cut out the summary page heart and paste it on the poster. This is an interactive way to help the reader see and celebrate the progress they are making as they complete the program.

The Heart's Way program can be done multiple times. Each time the reader will uncover yet a deeper layer of his or her heart.

This book will change every aspect of a reader's life, from lifestyle to relationships to chosen careers. Vince, a recovering intellectual client who completed the 12-week program said, "I was accomplished, financially sound and extremely depressed. After participating in Dr. Lamm's "Heart's Way" program I met the love of my life, discovered the purpose of my life, and began to live and breathe life as opposed to stumbling through it. This program did more to change my life than anything I have ever done."

Markets for the Book

There are approximately four markets for this book. Those markets are:

1) Business, corporate and non-profit executives and professionals who seek to grow beyond the confines of their limited lives (e.g., Those who have read books in the past – such as Tom Peters and Steven Covey);

2) Individuals currently seeking the counsel of therapists, coaches, ministers and physicians in regard to dealing with depression or unresolved personal issues in their lives;

3) Those who have flocked to and read books such as "The Artist's Way" and "The Purpose Driven Life;"

4) The spouses, family members, close friends, colleagues and employers of all of the above.

There is no religious orientation to this book – it is nondenominational. Each human being has a heart so anyone who wants a greater relationship with his or her heart will love this book. It is an inspiring way to open your heart and is guaranteed to save thousands of dollars in therapy and coaching bills.

Length and Completion Date

The final manuscript will be completed within 6 months of signing a contract with a publisher.

Spin-Offs

The author will write follow-up books:

Moving into the Heart's Way—This book will help readers transition into their new life after completing the Heart's Way program. It will facilitate long lasting behavior change.

Living the Heart's Way—A collection of stories from people who have made this transition, including descriptions of how their lives are so much better and how they keep living the Heart's Way each day.

Leading to the Heart's Way—A collection of stories on how readers from the previous books have led others in their lives to take steps to also live the Heart's Way.

In addition, the author will write complementary books to The Heart's Way such as:
Daily Inspiration For Living A Heart's Way Life: Reflections from the Heart's Way Program designed to be used as a convenient stand alone book for daily reflection or as an easy reference tool when reading The Heart's Way as well as customized journals for The Heart's Way and each of the above follow up books.

The Soul's Way—A book much like The Heart's Way but focused on following one's soul.
Promotional Plan

Mission Statement

Dr. Lamm's mission is to empower people from all races, belief systems, denominations and ages to reconnect with their hearts and live their divine purpose. This book is the next step. Dr. Lamm has pursued her mission through her award-winning research on personal transformation, speaking engagements, articles and book chapters, media appearances, and her private coaching practice.

Dr. Lamm has a solid platform she can leverage to promote the book and expand its impact. She has designed and delivered thousands of innovative programs and presentations around the world. She has coached hundreds of executives, entrepreneurs, professionals and CEO's. Through Dr. Lamm's speaking engagements, programs and coaching she is in front of at least 2,000 executives and professionals each year. Her client organizations include several Fortune 500 companies such as, GE, Boeing, and American Express. She also teaches at Columbia University and the Center for Creative Leadership and is the Director of Central Phoenix Women.

Dr. Lamm has been quoted in Oprah magazine as a personal transformation expert and written several journal articles and book chapters on the subject. Her doctorate dissertation on personal transformation received two distinguished awards for its innovative contribution to the field. Dr. Lamm's business was showcased on a Philadelphia local TV program as well as a National Cable TV program. She has been featured in the Phoenix Business Journal, Frontdoors newspaper, Desert Paradise Magazine, and several Who's Who publications.

The author will contribute to the promotion by the publisher in the following ways:

1. PR Budget. Dr. Lamm will match the publisher's consumer promotion budget up to $30,000

2. Media Campaign: Dr. Lamm will hire her own publicist to assist in the efforts of the publisher.

3. Blog Campaign: Dr. Lamm will direct her publicist under the guidance of the publisher to commence a Blog campaign to promote her book.

4. Tour: Dr. Lamm and her publicist, in conjunction with the efforts of the publisher, will set up a media/book signing campaign in the following cities. Dr. Lamm and/or her publicist will contact local newspapers, TV, radio stations, and women's organizations in several cities to set up interviews about her book. The cities will include Phoenix, Tucson, San Francisco, San Diego, Los Angeles, Portland, Seattle, New York, Philadelphia, Washington DC, Baltimore, Boston, Chicago, etc.

5. PBS: Dr. Lamm will utilize her already established connections with PBS in Phoenix as well as other PBS stations nationwide to drive promotional opportunities for her book

5. Teleconference Presentations: Dr. Lamm and her publicist will set up a minimum of 100 teleconference presentations featuring information and promotion on her book.

6. Seminars and Presentations: Dr. Lamm is in the process of designing specific seminars for the general public under the titles of "The Heart's Way," "Recovering Your Heart," and "Recovering Intellectuals Anonymous." She and her publicist will establish opportunities for her to present these classes at colleges, universities and organizations.

7. Organization Connections: Dr. Lamm will also be offering these presentations through a variety of Fortune 500 companies and businesses, such as GE's Leadership Development Center, Columbia University, ARCO

Chemical Company, Mobil, Exxon, Pepsi, E*TRADE, Stanley Tools, Syngenta, Storecast Merchandising, Fannie Mae, Arizona Society of CPA's, Boeing, American Express, Philadelphia School District, National Association of Women Business Owners—Sedona and Phoenix, Berlex Pharmaceuticals, Fannie Mae, Arizona Society of CPA's, Volvo Corporation, Holy Cross Hospital, and Fresh Start's Women's Resource Center.

8. Keynote Presentations: Dr. Lamm will continue her efforts as a keynote presenter at the following professional conferences: The Academy of Human Resource Development; Transformative Learning Conference; Arizona Women's Leadership Forum; etc.

9. Educational Programs: Dr. Lamm will continue her teaching efforts. She teaches at Columbia University and the Center for Creative Leadership and is the Director for a new Women's Leadership Organization—Central Phoenix Women.

10. Internet: Dr. Lamm and her publicist will employ the services of a professional web master to design and implement a web site which will supplement all of her other promotional efforts. Sharon will integrate the book with her business website www.insideoutlearninginc-,com and several other web sites in organizations that she subcontracts through and has client relationships with, including her client organizations described in #7 above and Columbia University. Sharon is well connected and will use these connections to promote her book through web site integrations.

11. Promotional copies: Dr. Lamm will send over 150 promotional autographed copies to existing and new media contacts as well as her corporate and organizational clients, universities and several women's organizations and encourage them to block-buy books for their employees, members and others.

12. Supporting Articles (including O Magazine): Dr. Lamm will utilize her already strong connection with Martha Beck who writes for O magazine to be potentially featured in that publication as well as Time, Newsweek, Business Week, Fortune and other journals.

13. Testimonials: Dr. Lamm will provide endorsements from people (many of whom she has personal connections with) such as: Deepok Chopra, Byron Katie, Marianne Williamson, Oprah, Martha Beck, Madonna, Wayne Dyer, Judith Orloff, Doreen Virtue, Melissa Ethridge, and Hilary and Bill Clinton.

Competing Books

The two international best-selling books that are most similar to The Heart's Way are Julia Cameron's, The Artist's Way and Rick Warren's The Purpose-Driven Life.

The Artist's Way is a 12-week program to recover our artist within. The main subject matter is around creativity. The Heart's Way is a 12-week program to recover your heart within. The main subject matter is re-connecting with your heart. Connecting with one's heart is much broader than creativity. The Heart's Way is for anyone who has lost touch with their heart and perhaps hidden their heart's authentic voice under a pilthora of accomplishments, achievements, invented personas and workaholic/busy life styles.

Julia Cameron proved that a 12-week structured self-help program is a best-selling methodology. It is still going strong after 10 years on the market. The Heart's Way provides a program that is more simple to use arranged around an acronym "Open Your Heart." One of the criticisms of Cameron's work is that there are just too many tasks to do. It adds to our stressful busy life styles instead of contributing to reducing them. Each week, The Heart's Way will provide journal exercises, a heart date, real-life stories of people who have completed each program week and a couple of stretch exercises for the overachieving audience this book will attract. It is incredibly easy and simple to use – its beauty is in its simplicity.

The Purpose-Driven Life is a 40-day structured program that the reader can use to connect with their unique purpose. Again a structured self-help program proves to make the international best-selling list. However, The Purpose-Driven Life is incredibly religious and connected with the Born Again Church. Even with the strong religious overtones of this book, it became a bestseller.

After searching databases of books with "Heart's Way" in the title, most have a religious connotation and none provide a simple program based on years of research and experience. The Heart's Way is a non-denominational book. Anyone from any religion will enjoy this book. There are no references to any religion. Each human being has a heart, regardless of their chosen religious orientation.

The Heart's Way is a uniquely powerful simple program that is vastly needed in our busy and "heady" society. It is guaranteed to be an international best seller.

About the Author

Dr. Sharon Lamm is an award-winning global coach, leadership development consultant, speaker, writer and educator. She is the President and founder of Inside-Out Learning, Inc., specializing in leadership and personal development, from the heart.

With over 18 years of global experience, Sharon has worked across the United States and Europe as well as Beijing, Hong Kong, Singapore and Thailand for clients such as American Express, GE's Leadership Development Center, Exxon, E*TRADE, ARCO Chemical Company, Mobil Oil Corporation, Berlex Pharmaceuticals, Fannie Mae, Arizona Society of CPA's, Volvo Corporation, Holy Cross Hospital, and Fresh Start Women's Resource Center.

She has designed and delivered thousands of innovative programs and has coached hundreds of CEO's, executives, educators, professionals and entrepreneurs worldwide. She is currently a preferred executive coach for American Express and Boeing.

In addition to her private practice, consulting and being on the global lecture circuit, she has published several journal articles and book chapters. She has also produced an audio CD workbook on Discovering your Purpose and is currently writing two books: 1) Rebirth Through Birth − Rediscovering Yourself Through Motherhood and 2) The Heart's Way.

Dr. Sharon Lamm is dedicated to community stewardship and has served with the Fresh Start Women's Foundation and Arizona State University's Dean's Board of Excellence Mentoring Program. In 2005 she was named as a woman to watch in the Phoenix Business Journal. She is the Director of a new Women's Leadership Organization − Central Phoenix Women.

Dr. Lamm holds a doctorate from Columbia University in Leadership and Organization Development, a Masters in Industrial and Labor Relations from Cornell University, and two Bachelor degrees. Sharon has trained as a Life Coach with world-renowned author and life coach teacher, Dr. Martha Beck. She is a Certified Executive and Leadership Coach and a Certified Teacher of the Myers Briggs Type Indicator.

Dr. Sharon Lamm is an adjunct professor of Leadership at Columbia University. She is an adjunct faculty member at the Center for Creative Leadership (San Diego Campus), which is consistently rated the #1 leadership development center.

Dr. Lamm has been honored and received awards from the Center for Creative Leadership and the Academy of Human Resource Development for her work and research on personal transformation and leadership development.

She was recently featured in Arizona's local Desert Paradise Magazine. She has been quoted on her views of coaching in the July, 2004 edition of Oprah's magazine, "O' magazine."

She lives just outside of Phoenix Arizona with her husband James Hartman and her son Joshua and cat Phoenix.

The Outline
List of Chapters

PART I: **Setting Context**

Introduction
& Quiz   Just How Much Of A Recovering
                    Intellectual Are You?

Chapter 1:   How to Use This Book to Recover Your
                    Heart

This Chapter describes how to use the book and variations for completing the 12-week program. The book can be done individually or as part of a group with two or more members. It can be completed multiple times uncovering new layers of one's heart each time. This Chapter sets individual and/or group expectations and goals for the program and provides references to the years of research the book is based upon.

PART II: **The 12-week Program—"Open Your Heart"**

Chapter 2:   "O" – Open to Receive

Chapter 3:   "P" – Purpose

Chapter 4:   "E" – Empathy

Chapter 5:   "N" – Nurturing

Chapter 6:   "Y" – You – Who are You?

Chapter 7:   "O" – Optimism

Chapter 8:   "U" – Unconditional

Sample Non-Fiction Proposal Package

CORN SUGAR AND BLOOD
Rick Porrello

OVERVIEW
When "Big Joe" Lonardo and his three brothers settled in Cleveland, they were followed here by the seven Porrello brothers, boyhood friends from Licata, Sicily. "Big Joe," backed by a fierce gang, eventually controlled much of the bootleg-related crime in northeast Ohio. Joe Porrello was a corporal in Lonardo's gang.

In 1925, Porrello left the Lonardos and organized his brothers who became corn sugar dealers like the Lonardos. When the Lonardos obtained a lock on the sugar business, they had only one competitor. You guessed it, their old friends the Porrellos.

Soon after "Big Joe" Lonardo left on a long trip to Sicily, the Porrellos began taking over Lonardo customers, growing prosperous and powerful in a short time. When "Big Joe" returned, a former Lonardo employee took advantage of the stormy situation and set up "Big Joe." His murder shocked the underworld and started a bitter campaign of revenge by the Lonardo family. In the process, another Lonardo brother was killed and four of the seven Porrello brothers died. This story was the bloodiest chapter in organized crime between Chicago and New York and made front-page headlines for five years. It is still featured occasionally in magazine and newspaper articles.

RESEARCH

I am a suburban Cleveland police officer and have been researching this story for over three years. Having grown accustomed to the raised eyebrows and wise guy comments, I now feel fortunate to admit that this fascinating piece of history is part of my family background. You see, my grandfather and his six brothers are among the main characters. I also feel fortunate to be the first person able to tell the story in its entirety.

With the exception of an unexpected need for further information, research for CORN SUGAR AND BLOOD has been completed. At my present pace, the story should be completed by the first months of 1993. Book length is estimated at 80,000 to 90,000 words. I have a collection of over 120 photographs available, many of which have never been viewed before by the public.

ABOUT THE AUTHOR

Rick Porrello is a Greater Cleveland police officer with Mafia roots. His grandfather and three uncles were mob leaders killed in Prohibition-era, bootleg violence. Porrello is an accomplished musician, having spent almost three years traveling worldwide as the drummer for the late Sammy Davis, Jr. Rick has a degree in criminal justice. He is married and lives in suburban Cleveland.

THE RISE AND FALL OF THE CLEVELAND MAFIA -
CORN SUGAR AND BLOOD

CHAPTER-BY-CHAPTER SYNOPSIS

Chapter 1: Birth of the Cleveland Mafia

During the late 1800s, the four Lonardo brothers and seven Porrello brothers were boyhood friends and fellow sulphur mine workers in their hometown of Licata, Sicily. They came to America in the early 1900s and eventually settled in the Woodland district of Cleveland. They remained close friends. Several of the Porrello and Lonardo brothers worked together in small businesses.

Lonardo clan leader "Big Joe" became a successful businessman and community leader in the lower Woodland Avenue area. During Prohibition, he became successful as a dealer in corn sugar, which was used by bootleggers to make corn liquor. "Big Joe" provided stills and raw materials to the poor Italian district residents. They would make the booze and "Big Joe" would buy it back, giving them a commission. He was respected and feared as a "padrone" or godfather. "Big Joe" became the leader of a powerful and vicious gang and was known as the corn sugar "baron." Joe Porrello was one of his corporals.

Chapter 2: The First Bloody Corner

With the advent of Prohibition, Cleveland, like other big cities, experienced a wave of bootleg-related murders. The murders of Louis Rosen, Salvatore Vella, August Rini, and several others produced the same suspects, but no indict ments. These suspects were members of the Lonardo gang. Several of the murders occurred at the corner of E. 25th and Woodland Ave. This intersection became known as the "bloody corner."

By this time, Joe Porrello had left the employ of the Lonardos to start his own sugar wholesaling business. Porrello and his six brothers pooled their money and eventually became successful corn sugar dealers headquartered in the upper Woodland Avenue area around E. 110th Street.

With small competitors, sugar dealers, and bootleggers mysteriously dying violent deaths, the Lonardo's business flourished as they gained a near monopoly on the corn sugar business. Their main competitors were their old friends the Porrellos.

Raymond Porrello, youngest of the brothers, was arrested by undercover federal agents for arranging a sale of 100 gallons of whiskey at the Porrello-owned barbershop at E. 110th and Woodland. He was sentenced to the Dayton, Ohio, Workhouse.

The Porrello brothers paid the influential "Big Joe" Lonardo $5,000 to get Raymond out of prison. "Big Joe" failed in his attempt but never returned the $5,000.

Meanwhile, Ernest Yorkell and Jack Brownstein, small-time, self-proclaimed "tough guys" from Philadelphia, arrived in Cleveland. Yorkell and Brownstein were shakedown artists, and their intended victims were Cleveland bootleggers, who got a chuckle out of how the two felt it necessary to explain that they were tough. Real tough guys didn't need to tell people that they were tough. After providing Cleveland gangsters with a laugh, Yorkell and Brownstein were taken on a "one-way ride."

Chapter 3: Corn Sugar and Blood

"Big Joe" Lonardo, in 1926, now at the height of his wealth and power, left for Sicily to visit his mother and relatives. He left his closest brother and business partner John in charge.

During "Big Joe's" six-month absence, he lost much of his $5,000-a-week profits to the Porrellos, who took advantage of John Lonardo's lack of business skills and gained the assistance of a disgruntled Lonardo employee. "Big Joe" returned and business talks between the Porrellos and Lonardos began. They "urged" the Porrellos to return their lost clientele.

On October 13, 1927, "Big Joe" and John Lonardo went to the Porrello barbershop to play cards and talk business with Angelo Porrello, as they had been doing for the past week. As the Lonardos entered the rear room of the shop, two gunmen opened fire. Angelo Porrello ducked under a table.

Cleveland's underworld lost its first boss as "Big Joe" went down with three bullets in his head. John Lonardo was shot in the chest and groin but drew his gun and managed to pursue the attackers through the barbershop. He dropped his gun in the shop but continued chasing the gunmen into the street where one of them turned and, out of bullets, struck Lonardo in the head several times with the butt of his gun. John fell unconscious and bled to death.

The Porrello brothers were arrested. Angelo was charged with the Lonardo brothers' murders. The charges were later dropped for lack of evidence. Joe Porrello succeeded the Lonardos as corn sugar "baron" and later appointed himself "capo" of the Cleveland Mafia.

Chapter 4: The Cleveland Meeting

The trail of bootleg blood continued to flow with numerous murders stemming from the Porrello-Lonardo conflict.

Lawrence Lupo, a former Lonardo bodyguard, was killed after he let it be known that he wanted to take over the Lonardo's corn sugar business.

Anthony Caruso, a butcher who saw the Lonardos' killers escape, was shot and killed. It was believed that he knew the identities of the gunmen and was going to reveal them to police.

On December 5, 1928, Joe Porrello and his lieutenant and bodyguard Sam Tilocco hosted the first known major meeting of the Mafia at Cleveland's Hotel Statler. Many major Mafia leaders from Chicago to New York to Florida were invited. The meeting was raided before it actually began. Joe Profaci, leader of a Brooklyn, N.Y., Mafia family, was the most well-known of the gangsters arrested. He was the founder of the Colombo Mafia family. Vincent Mangano also ranked high as founder of the Gambino family, most recently headed by the "Dapper Don" John Gotti.

Within a few hours, to the astonishment of police and court officials, Joe Porrello gathered 30 family members and friends who put up their houses as collateral for the gangsters' bonds. Profaci was bailed out personally by Porrello. A great controversy over the validity of the bonds followed.

Several theories have been given as to why the meeting was called. First, it was thought that the gangsters, local presidents of the Unione Siciliane, an immigrant aid society infiltrated by the Mafia, were there to elect a new national president. Their previous president Frankie Yale had been recently killed by order of Chicago's notorious Al Capone. Second, it was believed that the meeting may have been called to organize the highly lucrative corn sugar industry. It was also said that the men were there to "confirm" Joe Porrello as "capo" of Cleveland.

Capone, a non-Sicilian, was reported to be in Cleveland for the meeting. He left soon after his arrival at the advice of associates who said that the Sicilians did not want him there.

Chapter 5: The Second Bloody Corner

As Joe Porrello's power and wealth grew, heirs and close associates to the Lonardo brothers grew hot for revenge.

Angelo Lonardo, "Big Joe's" 18-year-old son along with his mother and his cousin, drove to the corner of E. 110th and Woodland, the Porrello stronghold. There Angelo sent word that his mother wanted to speak to Salvatore "Black Sam" Todaro. Todaro, now a Porrello lieutenant, had worked for Angelo's father and was believed to be responsible for his murder. In later years, it was believed that he was actually one of the gunmen.

As Todaro approached to speak with Mrs. Lonardo, whom he respected, Angelo pulled out a gun and emptied it into "Black Sam's" stocky frame. Todaro crumpled to the sidewalk and died.

Angelo and his cousin disappeared for several months, reportedly being hid in Chicago courtesy of Lonardo friend Al Capone. Later, it was believed that Angelo spent time in California with his uncle Dominick, the fourth Lonardo brother who fled west when indicted for a payroll robbery murder in 1921.

Eventually, Angelo and his cousin were arrested and

charged with "Black Sam's" murder. For the first time in Cleveland's bootleg murder history, justice was served as both young men were convicted and sentenced to life. Justice, although served, would be short-lived as they would be released only a year and a half later after winning a new trial.

Chapter 6: Rise of the Mayfield Road Mob
On October 20, 1929, Frank Lonardo, brother to "Big Joe" and John, was shot to death while playing cards. Two theories were given for his death: that it was in revenge for the murder of "Black Sam" Todaro; and that he was killed for not paying gambling debts. Mrs. Frank Lonardo, when told of her husband's murder, screamed, "I'll get them. I'll get them myself if I have to kill a whole regiment!"

By 1929, Little Italy crime boss Frank Milano had risen to power as leader of his own gang, "The Mayfield Road Mob." Milano's group was made up in part of remnants of the Lonardo gang and was also associated with the powerful "Cleveland Syndicate," Morrie Kleinman, Moe Dalitz, Sam Tucker, and Louis Rothkopf. The Cleveland Syndicate was responsible for most of the Canadian booze imported via Lake Erie. In later years, they got into the casino business. One of their largest and most profitable enterprises was construction of the Desert Inn Hotel/Casino in Las Vegas. Dalitz would become known as the "Godfather of Las Vegas." He would be murdered in 1986 as part of a Mafia war for control of Las Vegas.

Joe Porrello admired Milano's political organization, the East End Bi-Partisan Political Club, and, seeing the value in such influence, wanted to ally himself with the group. Milano refused. Later, Porrello was reported to have affiliated himself with the newly formed 21st District Republican Club. He hoped to organize the Woodland Avenue voters as Milano was doing on Mayfield Road.

Chapter 7: More Corn Sugar and Blood

By 1930, Milano had grown quite powerful. He had gone so far as to demand a piece of the lucrative Porrello corn sugar business. On July 5, 1930, Porrello received a phone call from Milano who had requested a conference at his Venetian Restaurant on Mayfield Road. Sam Tilocco and Joe Porrello's brother Raymond urged him not to go.

At about 2:00 p.m., Joe Porrello and Sam Tilocco arrived at Milano's restaurant and speakeasy. Porrello, Tilocco, and Frank Milano sat down in the restaurant and discussed business. Several of Milano's henchmen sat nearby. The atmosphere was tense as Porrello refused to accede to Milano's demands.

Porrello reached into his pocket for his watch to check the time. Two of Milano's men, possibly believing that Porrello was reaching for his gun, opened fire. With three bullets in his head, Porrello died instantly. Simultaneously, a third member of Milano's gang fired at Tilocco, who was struck three times but managed to stagger out the door toward his new Cadillac. He fell to the ground as the gunmen pursued him, finishing him off with another six bullets.

Frank Milano and several of his restaurant employees were arrested but only charged with being suspicious persons. The gunmen were never actually identified. Only one witness was present in the saloon when the shooting started. He was Frank Joiner, a slot machine distributor whose only testimony was that he "thought" he saw Frank Milano in the restaurant during the murders.

Cleveland's aggressive and outspoken Safety Director Edwin Barry, frustrated by the continually rising number of bootleg murders, ordered all known sugar warehouses to be padlocked. He ordered a policeman to be detailed at each one to make sure that no sugar was brought in or removed.

Meanwhile, the six Porrello brothers donned black silk shirts and ties and buried their most successful brother. The showy double gangster funeral was one of the largest Cleveland had ever seen. Two bands and 33 cars overloaded with flowers led the procession of the slain don and his bodyguard. Over 250 automobiles containing family and friends followed. Thousands of mourners and curious onlookers lined the sidewalks.

Cleveland's underworld was tense with rumors of imminent warfare. Porrello's brother Vincente-James spoke openly of wiping out everyone responsible for his brother's murder.

Three weeks after his brother's murder, Jim Porrello still wore a black shirt as he entered the I & A grocery and meat market at E. 110th Street and Woodland. As he picked out lamb chops at the meat counter, a Ford touring car, its curtains tightly drawn, cruised slowly past the store. A couple of shotguns poked out and two thunderous blasts of buckshot were fired, one through the front window of the store and one through the front screen door.

The amateur gunmen got lucky. Two pellets found the back of Porrello's head and entered his brain. He was rushed to the hospital.

Chapter 8: "I think maybe they'll kill all us Porrellos."

"I think maybe they'll kill all us Porrellos. I think maybe they will kill all of us except Rosario. They can't kill him - he's in jail." Thus, Ottavio Porrello grimly but calmly predicted the probable fate of him and his brothers as he waited outside Jim's hospital room.

Next to Ottavio was a tough looking young man who smoked cigarettes and blew the smoke at the hospital's No Smoking signs. It was said he was a bodyguard, something the Porrellos never employed enough of. Jim Porrello died at 5:55 p.m.

Two local petty gangsters were arrested and charged with murder. One was discharged by directed verdict, and the other was acquitted. Like almost all of Cleveland's bootleg-related murders, the killers never saw justice.

About this time, it was rumored that the Porrello brothers were marked for extermination. The surviving brothers went into hiding. Raymond, known for his cocky attitude and hot temper, spoke like his brother James did of seeking revenge. Raymond was smarter though, he took active measures to protect himself.

On August 15, 1930, three weeks after James Porrello's murder, Raymond Porrello's house was leveled in a violent explosion. He was not home at the time, since he had taken his family and abandoned his home in anticipation of the attack.

Four days later, Frank Alessi, a witness to the murder of "Big Joe" Lonardo's brother Frank, was gunned down. From his deathbed, he identified Frank Brancato as his assailant. Brancato was known mainly as a Lonardo supporter and suspect in several murders. Brancato was acquitted of Alessi's murder.

Chapter 9: This shooting was Cleveland's deadliest
Mob hit ever.

In March of 1931, Rosario Porrello was paroled from
Ohio's London Prison Farm where he had served one year for
carrying a gun in his car.

In mid-1931, National Mafia "capo di tutti capi" (boss of
all bosses) Salvatore Maranzano was killed. His murder set in
motion the formation of the first Mafia National Ruling
Commission, created to stop the numerous murders
resulting from conflicts between and within Mafia families
and to promote application of modern business practices to
crime.

Charles "Lucky" Luciano was the main developer of the
commission and was named chairman. Also named to the
commission were Al Capone of Chicago, Joe Profaci of
Brooklyn, and Frank Milano of Cleveland.

In December of 1931, Angelo Lonardo and his cousin
Dominic Suspirato were released from prison after being
acquitted of "Black Sam" Todaro's murder during a second
trial. Because he had avenged his father's death and (for the
most part) gotten away with it, he became a respected
member of Frank Milano's Mayfield Road Mob.

The thirst for revenge had not been satisfied for members
of the Lonardo family. It was generally believed that "Black
Sam" Todaro instigated and perhaps took part in the murders
of "Big Joe" and John Lonardo. However, it was believed by
members of the Lonardo family that the remaining Porrello
brothers, particularly the volatile John and Raymond and
eldest brother Rosario, still posed a threat because of the
murders of Joe and James Porrello.

On February 25, 1932, Raymond Porrello, his brother

Rosario, and their bodyguard Dominic Gulino (known also by several aliases) were playing cards near E. 110th and Woodland Avenue. The front door burst open and, in a hail of bullets, the Porrello brothers, their bodyguard, and a bystander went down. The Porrellos died at the scene. Gulino died a couple of hours later. The bystander eventually recovered from his wounds. This shooting was Cleveland's deadliest Mob hit ever.

Several hours after the murders, Frank Brancato, with a bullet in his stomach, dragged himself into St. John's Hospital on Cleveland's west side. He claimed he was shot in a street fight on the west side. A few days later, tests on the bullet taken from Brancato revealed that it came from a gun found at the Porrello brothers' murder scene. Although never convicted of either of the murders, Brancato was convicted of perjury for lying to a Grand Jury about his whereabouts during the murder. He served four years after a one- to ten-year sentence was commuted by Governor Martin L. Davey.

In 1933, Prohibition was repealed. The bootleg murders mostly stopped as organized crime moved into other enterprises. Angelo Lonardo continued his crime career as a respected member of the Cleveland family, eventually rising through the ranks to run the northeast Ohio rackets in 1980.

Chapter 10: "Big Ange" and the Death of the Cleveland Mafia

In 1983, Angelo Lonardo, 72, one-time Cleveland Mafia boss, turned government informant. He shocked family, friends, law enforcement officers, and, particularly, criminal associates with his decision, which was made after being sentenced to life plus 103 years for drug and racketeering convictions. The sentence came after a monumental investigation into the murder of the greatly feared Mafia enemy Danny Greene. The complex plot to kill "The Irishman" involved Mafia members from, and associated with, Erie, New York, Youngstown, Akron, and the West Coast.

"Big Ange" as he was called, was the highest ranking mafioso to defect. He testified in 1985 at the Las Vegas casino "skimming" trials in Kansas City and in 1986 at the New York Mafia "ruling commission" trials. Many of the nation's most powerful mob leaders, including Tony Salerno, boss of the Genovese crime family, were convicted as a result of these trials.

(Rick's book, *The Rise and Fall of the Cleveland Mafia* was eventually published by Barricade Books. He went on to publish a second book, *To Kill the Irishman: The War That Crippled the Mafia*, which has gone into a second printing and has also been optioned for a movie.)

To get in touch with

Tom Bird

explore his services or find
and when he will be teaching,
either visit his website at:

www.TomBird.com

or call his office at:

928-203-0265

Printed in the United States
204748BV00004B/367-402/A